TOP 100 HOT-SPOTS FOR SEA FISHES IN AUSTRALIA

TOP 100 HOT-SPOTS FOR

A Fishwatching Guide for Divers, Snorkellers and Naturalists

SEA FISHES IN AUSTRALIA

Nigel Marsh

Contents

ACKNOWLEDGEMENTS

The author has spent more than 40 years exploring the seas around Australia while fishwatching, and would like to thank the following people and dive operators for support in making this book possible.

Queensland: Mike Ball (Mike Ball Dive Expeditions), Spirit of Freedom, Phillip Hobbs and Trina Baker, James McVeigh (Big Cat Reality), Megan Bell (Quicksilver Group), Greg Laurent (Kiana Charters), Heron Island Resort, Lady Elliot Eco Resort, Lady Musgrave Cruises, Julian Negri (Bundaberg Aqua Scuba), Fiona and James Skilbeck Nelson (Wolf Rock Dive), Mike McKinnon (Scubaworld), Dan Hart (Sunreef Diving Services), Lisa Edwards (Nautilus Supercat), James Griffith (Manta Lodge and Scuba Centre), Mark Robertson (Go Dive), Steve Rossberg (Brisbane Scuba) and Harry Cottrell, Seb Lovera and Mitch Bennett (Gold Coast Dive Adventures).

New South Wales: Andrew Trevor-Jones, Chris Mair (Ocean Dive Charters), Rod and Christina Gray (Blue Bay Divers), Giacomo Cavazzini (Sundive), Chris Connell (Dive Quest), Mike and Deb Davey (Jetty Dive Centre), Jon Cragg (Fish Rock Dive Centre), Ron Hunter (Dive Forster), Dive Jervis Bay, Darryl Stuart (Narooma Charters), Martin and Cathie Thackray (Montague Island Charters) and Merimbula Divers Lodge.

Victoria: Mary Malloy, Allie Beckhurst, Margaret Flierman and Geoffrey Whitehorn.

Tasmania: Bicheno Dive Centre, Mick Baron and Karen Gowlett-Holmes (Eaglehawk Dive Centre) and Ian Palmer (The Dive Shop Hobart).

South Australia: Carey Harmer (Sea Optics) and Andrew Fox (Rodney Fox Shark Expeditions).

Western Australia: Peter MacDonald (The Dive Shed), Uwe Klinge and Liane Sulkowski, Kim Royce, Andrew McGuckin (Lionfish Charters Perth), Greg Lowry, Kristin Anderson, Peter Trembath (North Star Cruises), Exmouth Diving Centre and David Watchorn (Christmas Island Extra Divers).

And finally, fish scientist Jeff Johnson, Mark McGrouther, Doug Hoese and Rudie Kuiter.

DEDICATION

*To Susan Vandervalk
and to my wonderful wife Helen Rose,
my favourite fishwatching buddy.*

Nigel Marsh is an Australian underwater photographer and photojournalist whose work has been published in numerous magazines, newspapers and books all around the world. Nigel has dived extensively around Australia, and also throughout Asia, the Pacific Ocean, the Indian Ocean and the Caribbean. His underwater photographs have won a number of international photographic awards. Nigel has written over a dozen books on diving and marine related subjects, including titles for New Holland such as *Diving With Sharks, Underwater Australia* and *Muck Diving*.

INTRODUCTION

Australia is blessed with an abundance of fishes. More than 5,000 species are found Down Under – around 15 per cent of the known species – making Australia one of the best places in the world to see fishes, and lots of them.

Australia has such a rich variety of fishes because of the diverse range of habitats found around this vast island nation. From its warm tropical waters in the north to its cool temperate waters in the south, fishes populate every available aquatic environment – rivers, mangroves, estuaries, coral reefs, rocky reefs, kelp forests, seagrass beds, sandy plains and even the deep ocean.

Many of Australia's tropical fish species are shared with other countries in the Indo-Pacific region. However, once you head south, into subtropical and temperate waters, things change dramatically, as these zones are filled with endemic species – fishes found nowhere else on the planet. These cooler waters are where you can encounter seadragons, handfish, prowfish, blue devils and many other unique Australian fishes. Fishes that attract divers and snorkellers from around the world to plunge Down Under.

This book is the first guide to fishwatching in Australia. Now fishwatching may be a new term for most people, but just like birdwatching it best describes what divers, snorkellers and naturalists do when they study, observe and document fishes. This book is designed especially for the fishwatcher. It is intended as a sort of blending of a fish identification guide and a dive site guide, resulting in a unique guide to the best spots to observe sea fishes in Australia.

Each of the 100 hot-spots I have chosen is home to a diverse range of fishes, and for each I have listed a sample of typical fish species and families that can be seen. However, most of these hot-spots have been selected because they are also the best place to observe unusual fishes.

Throughout the pages of this book you will learn about the wonderful fishes of Australia, the best places to see them, how to find them, and how to get close enough to observe and photograph them.

Above: Seadragons are only found in Australian waters, with the Weedy Seadragon a wide-ranging species in temperate waters.

Below: The Southern Blue Devil is a unique endemic Aussie fish.

WHAT IS FISHWATCHING?

I may not have invented the term fishwatching, but it is a name that I started to use during the pandemic. Stuck in lockdown, like many Australians, and with restricted movement, I couldn't explore Australia's underwater world looking for fishes. Still needing a wildlife fix, I found myself rediscovering my love of birdwatching. I quickly found myself turning into a twitcher, documenting the local bird species I saw, and visiting new spots in the neighbourhood each week hoping to see and photograph birds I hadn't seen before.

While doing this, it suddenly dawned on me that I had been doing the same thing underwater for 40 years, except with fishes. I document all the fish species I see and photograph, I am always looking out for fishes I have never seen before and I travel around Australia looking to see new and exotic fishes. I was a fishwatcher and hadn't even realised it.

Fish, in my opinion, are far more varied and interesting than birds. For a start there are many more fish species in Australia than birds; 5,000 compared to 850. Fish also come in a much wider variety of shapes, colours and sizes. Plus, they also have much more interesting sex lives (how many birds change sex?). And on any hour-long dive anywhere in Australia I can guarantee you will see many more fish species than you would bird species during a week spent at the best birdwatching sites in the country.

Fishwatching is very entertaining, as fish are always busy feeding, fighting, defending, guarding, mating, displaying, cleaning, hiding, stalking, creeping, crawling, resting and sleeping, and they also interact with other marine life and divers. However, fishwatching is also very important for us to learn more about these wonderful animals.

We still know very little about most fish species. Fishes that are important to the seafood industry have been heavily studied, but most have never been looked at by marine researchers. The late, great Australian marine naturalist Neville Coleman OAM once told me: "Any diver that observes an Australian fish for more than an

Above: Photographs taken by divers have helped researchers studying the endangered Grey Nurse Shark.

Below: Australia's temperate waters are home to many unusual species, such as the Common Stargazer.

hour is probably the world expert on that fish!" This is because there is so little funding for fish research in Australia.

Fortunately, things have changed over the last decade with the growth of citizen science. Today divers, snorkellers and naturalists are asked to help researchers gather data. The simplest way this is done is by sharing images you take while diving and snorkelling. In Australia people are asked to share images of manta rays, Grey Nurse Sharks, Leopard Sharks and many other species. The sharing of these images has assisted researchers in ascertaining populations, migration patterns and important habitats for these species.

Other citizen-science projects you can share fish images to include iNaturalist, Red Maps and Eye on the Reef. Australasian Fishes is a particularly worthwhile project on iNaturalist, and a great asset to help you identify fishes. I often use this site to find where people have been seeing rare and unusual Australian fishes.

Fishwatching is a very rewarding experience, and with more than 5,000 species of fishes in Australian waters, and around 50 new species described each year, there are a great deal of fishy friends to be watched.

SORTING AUSTRALIAN FISH NAMES

Australian slang, or Strine, is known around the world for the way Aussies shorten and modify words. Many Australian words leave visitors from overseas confused and confounded, and this also includes some of our common names for fishes. Expect to hear fish names such as wobby (wobbegong), kingie (Yellowtail Kingfish), PJ (Port Jackson Shark), yakka (Yellowtail Scad), GT (Giant Trevally) and toadie (toadfish or pufferfish). However, in Australia we have also changed the names of some fish families, just to make things complicated.

Most fish have at least one common name, but some can have dozens. Common names are fine for most divers, snorkellers and naturalists, and have been used in this book. However, to avoid confusion between scientists when discussing fish,

Above: The Tasselled Frogfish is endemic to southern Australia. It is also known as the Tasselled Angler or Tasselled Anglerfish.

Below: The Bluespotted Pufferfish (*Omegophora cyanopunctata*) is also commonly called the Bluespotted Toadfish.

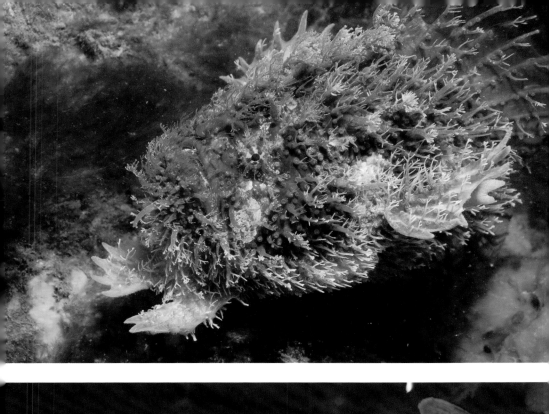

all fish have a single Latin scientific name based on a system known as binominal nomenclature. This system was invented by the Swedish botanist Carolus Linnaeus in 1785. Before his time the naming of plants and animals was a random mess, so Linnaeus brought order to the chaos by arranging all plants and animals into taxonomic divisions. These break down to Kingdom, Phylum, Class, Order, Family, Genus and finally Species.

Fish are members of the Kingdom Animalia (animals) and in the Phylum Chordata (animals with a backbone). However, when it comes to Class, the fish split into two camps, the Chondrichthyes (sharks, rays and chimaeras, which all have a skeleton made of cartilage) and the Osteichthys (the bony fishes). From there fishes get broken down further into Subclasses, Orders and Families, all based on similar body shapes and other characteristics.

Australian waters are home to more than 120 fish families, and this is where the common-name confusion starts. In Australia what we know as batfish are called spadefish in some countries. The same goes for leatherjackets, known as filefish elsewhere, and trevally, known as jacks in other countries. In this book I have kept the common Australian names for these fish families. However, for anglerfish, frogfish and toadfish, I have adopted the more commonly used international names, as the Australian use of these names is a little confusing.

Anglerfish are fish with head lures and are placed in the order Lophiiformes. Within this order are 16 different family groups, including the handfish (Brachionichthyidae) and the frogfish (Antennariidae). For some strange reason some Australians call frogfish anglerfish. It is confusing and only gets worse, as the name frogfish is instead used for the toadfish family (Batrachoididae). And then toadfish is used for some members of the pufferfish family (Tetraodontidae). Fortunately, many Australian divers use the more widely accepted internationally recognised names for these families, which is a change for the better.

Family names do change occasionally, and this has happened quite a bit in the last few years due to fish researchers using DNA technology to study them at a molecular level. One group that changed dramatically was the shovelnose rays. What

Above: The Broad Cowtail Stingray (*Pastinachus ater*) is a quite distinctive stingray species, and is one of many rays mistakenly called a Bull Ray.

Below: Even though there are ten quite different species of wobbegong found around Australia, such as this Banded Wobbegong, most are simply called a 'wobby'.

was once thought to be two families of these rays is now split into four: wedgefishes (Rhinidae), guitarfishes (Rhinobatidae), giant guitarfishes (Glaucostegidae) and banjo rays (Trygonorrhinidae). This has also happened in other families, and when this change occurs it takes longer for the common names to be revised and updated. One member of the wedgefish family seen in Australia is the Whitespotted Wedgefish. Confusingly it is still known by its old names – Whitespotted Guitarfish or Whitespotted Shovelnose Ray.

Most fish common names are widely used in Australia, so divers and snorkellers are mostly using the same language on the east, west and south coasts. However, there are a few exceptions, with the Banded Wobbegong (*Orectolobus halei*) a prime example. When this and its relative the Ornate Wobbegong (*Orectolobus ornatus*) were finally recognised as two different species, we ended up with an assortment of common names. The Banded Wobbegong is also called the Gulf, Halei's or Ornate Wobbegong, while some started to call the Ornate Wobbegong, which retained its scientific name, the Dwarf Ornate Wobbegong.

One of the most confusing common names you will hear is Bull Ray. I am not sure of the origin of this name, but suspect that it came from European divers as there is a species called the Bull Ray in the Mediterranean. However, in Australia this is not a common name for any ray species. Unfortunately, it seems to have been adopted by some Aussie divers to describe any stingray or eagle ray. I have heard it being used to describe seven different ray species, in both tropical and temperate waters, and all these rays look very different. Therefore Bull Ray is a name best avoided.

While I have used common names throughout this book, in the captions I have also included the scientific names for the 300 fish species that have been featured. It can take many years to learn fish names, and if you get familiar with the fish body shapes and can narrow down the family group you are on the road to becoming a good fishwatcher.

Opposite: Leafy Seadragon is one of the most highly sought-after fishes in southern Australia.

FINDING UNUSUAL FISHES

A great variety of unique and unusual fishes can be found around Australia. Some of these special species are abundant and easy to find, while others are rarely seen due to their cryptic nature, limited range or limited numbers. To find these special fishes a little research and planning is required, and also a lot of hard work and a dash of luck.

To start with you need to know as much as you can about the fish, especially where it is most likely to be found within its known range. This will put you in the right area. However, you also need to know the fish's preferred habitat – such as reef, seagrass, kelp, sand, estuary, shallow water, deep water, sheltered water or areas with current. Other important things to know are whether the fish is nocturnal or diurnal, and if the species is seasonal, only being seen at certain times of the year when it migrates to the area. Also is the fish active, seen swimming around the reef, or passive, resting on the bottom or hiding in caves, ledges, burrows or under the sand. Finally, local knowledge is invaluable, so contact local dive shops or divers who know the area well and will give sound advice on finding unusual fishes.

One of the most highly-prized Australian fishes is the magnificent Leafy Seadragon. Finding one of these spectacular fish is not too difficult, if you have the right advice and knowledge, and follow it. They are found off South Australia and southern Western Australia in sheltered bays with kelp and seagrass. However, my first attempts to find one in the early 1990s ended in failure, even though I dived sites in the right area with the right habitat. I thought I was clever enough to

The Colclough's Shark is a rarely seen endemic species.

find one myself, without seeking local assistance, and I went home empty handed. I learned from that trip to seek local knowledge, as local divers know the hot-spots where these magnificent fish are found.

Actually, the Leafy Seadragon is one of the easier unusual fish to find, as they are popular with divers, so most local divers and dive shops know the best spots to see them and whether they have been seen recently. However, I would recommend diving with a local guide to point them out, as they are incredibly hard to spot when swimming among seaweed.

Finding rarer and more obscure fishes is more of a challenge. A good example of this was my search for a Colclough's Shark. When I moved from Sydney to Brisbane in 1990, I had a list of fish species I wanted to see in this subtropical region, and top of that list was a Colclough's Shark. This endemic shark is only found off northern New South Wales and southern Queensland. However, so little was known about it that no one had even photographed one before. The only thing I knew about the shark was that it was related to the more common Blind Shark, which is a nocturnal hunter and hides under ledges by day. I had to assume that Colclough's Shark was similar.

Speaking to local divers and dive shops, it transpired that no one had ever seen one, in fact most didn't even know the shark existed. For two years I dived every local dive site searching for one of these little sharks, looking in every nook and cranny.

My long search finally paid off when I found one resting in a gutter at Shag Rock off Brisbane. I was overjoyed and shot plenty of images – the first-ever photos of this rare shark. Since then I have only found four more Colclough's Sharks, so they are extremely rare and to this day little is known about this secretive species.

Over the years I have searched for many unique and unusual fishes around Australia. Sometimes I have been lucky and found the fish quickly, other times it has taken me years to locate my target, and there are still plenty of species I have so far failed to find. Many of my best fish discoveries have been pure luck. In these instances, it helps to know your fishes and know what you are looking at is rare, unusual or even undescribed. I have had several great experiences like this. Such as the time I found an Australian Butterfly Ray in Moreton Bay, or a Barred Snakemoray at Great Detached Reef, or a Glauert's Frogfish off Bunbury.

However, one of my best fish finds was when diving the Navy Pier at Exmouth in 2006. It had been a brilliant dive, overloaded with fishes, when I found a strange velvetfish I had never seen before. I took several images, and then had quite a challenge discovering what the fish was. Neither Neville Coleman nor Rudie Kuiter, two of Australia's top fish experts, knew what the fish was, and both assumed it was undescribed. This turned out to be the case as the fish was a Goatee Velvetfish, which was not described until 2012. Unfortunately, the fish had been seen a few years before I found it, so I can't say that I discovered it.

Sadly, finding some fishes is becoming harder as they become rarer. Habitat loss, overfishing, pollution, invasive species and even rising sea temperatures from climate change have impacted many fish species around the country. None more so than the handfishes – a group of strange fish only found in southern Australia. These wonderful little fish, that walk on modified fins, are all critically endangered. Their numbers were probably always small, being ambush predators with a limited range. However, they have almost been wiped out by the invasive Pacific Sea Star eating their eggs.

Finding unusual fishes is an exciting and rewarding experience, and with so little known about most Australian fishes you might even discover a new species.

Left: Only found off northern Western Australia, the Goatee Velvetfish was undescribed when this image was taken in 2006.

Right: The bizarre Spotted Handfish is critically endangered, with only a small population found near Hobart.

PHOTOGRAPHING FISHES

Birdwatching and fishwatching are similar in many ways, and most people who take part in these activities also like to photograph their subjects. However, photographing fishes is very different to photographing birds.

Bird photography is mostly done with a telephoto lens, with the subject often 10m or more away from the photographer, and the great majority of these images are taken with natural light. Photographing fish is the complete opposite, with photographers using either a macro or wide-angle lens, generally with the subject only 1m away or closer and the great majority of images are taken with a strobe (flash). This is because when shooting through water light and detail is quickly absorbed, so the photographer must be as close as possible to the subject in order to get a clear and colourful picture.

Underwater photography has increased dramatically in popularity with the rise of digital technology. No longer restricted to 36 images on a roll of film, divers and snorkellers can now take unlimited digital photos while underwater and share them online with family, friends and complete strangers. Fish are among the most popular subjects for underwater photographers. However, getting good fish photos can be a challenge without the right gear, technique and of course the main ingredient – the fish.

Divers and snorkellers have access to a wide range of cameras that can be placed in watertight housings to be taken underwater. The simplest models are the compact cameras. These are cheap, easy to use, and while they have a fixed zoom lens, you can photograph large and small subjects with the addition of wet lenses. However, they do have their limits, with most having no manual settings, and worse, they all have a slight shutter delay, which makes it harder to photograph moving subjects such as reef fishes.

The next step up the ladder are the DSLR and Mirrorless cameras. These are more expensive, and require more time to master, but they produce much better results, especially with fish photography. These cameras allow you to change lenses. However, this results in you being stuck with the same lens the entire time you are underwater. Beside the cost, they are also much larger, which can make them more awkward to handle underwater in some situations.

Lens choice is critical for good fish photography. The standard zoom lens that comes with a compact camera, or a DSLR or mirrorless kit lens, is a good starting

Above: Some morays are easy to approach and photograph, while others are very shy. Fortunately this Lipspot Moray (*Gymnothorax chilospilus*) was quite curious.

Below: Some reef fishes are nervous and hard to approach, while others such as this Fanbelly Leatherjacket (*Monacanthus chinensis*) allow photographers to get very close.

Above: Small angelfish, like the rarely seen Herald's Angelfish (*Centropyge heraldi*), are typically camera shy and require patience in order to get successful photos.

Below: Schooling fish, such as these Goldstripe Goatfish (*Mulloidichthys vanicolensis*), are often easy to photograph as they are more confident being in a group.

point. These lenses generally allow you to photograph a range of small to medium-sized fishes – everything from a seahorse to a wobbegong. These are great lenses if you don't know what you are going to see.

A macro lens is required for tiny fish, and is also good for small fish. With a compact camera you can add a macro wet lens that attaches to the housing, which can then be taken off if a larger fish is spotted. However, when using a macro lens on a DSLR or mirrorless camera you will be stuck with it. My favourite macro lens for fish photography is the Nikon 60mm lens. Many of the photos in this book were taken with that lens, which allows for 1:1 images of tiny fish such as pygmy seahorses, but still allows for small fish, up to 40cm long, to be captured.

For larger fish, especially gropers, sharks and rays, a wide-angle lens is required. With a compact camera this once again requires a wet lens, while with a DSLR or mirrorless camera it is a dedicated wide-angle lens. Although these lenses have a wider view, the trick to using one is to get as close to the subject as possible.

Lighting is also critically important with underwater photography, as the water leaches out the colours. To bring back those colours you need to add a strobe or video light. As these are only effective for one to two metres through water, you need to get close to your subjects to light them properly. Some divers love video lights for photography, as they can also use them to do video. I personally prefer a strobe, as I find that video lights often frighten skittish fish away before you get a chance to take a photo. And studies have shown that even sensitive fish, such as seahorses, are unaffected by the flash of a strobe. However, they still don't appreciate the attention from a nosey photographer.

On a typical dive or snorkel you will see hundreds of fish doing hundreds of different things. Some sit on the bottom, others swim around the reef, some drift slowly with the current, others hover above the bottom, some dart in and out of a lair, others hang out of holes.

The easiest subjects are the stationary fish – ones that sit, rest, perch, sleep or attach to the bottom. These fit into two categories, the confident camouflages and the nervous Nellies. The first group are typically camouflaged and are so confident they are well hidden they allow you to get very close. These stationary subjects include morays, seahorses, seadragons, pipefish, ghostpipefish, scorpionfish, prowfish, frogfish, handfish, toadfish, velvetfish, lionfish, clingfish, lizardfish, gobies, blennies, threefins, dragonets, sea moths, stargazers, flounders, soles, wobbegongs, blind sharks, angel sharks, hornsharks, bamboo sharks and electric rays.

The nervous Nellies also rest on the bottom. However, they often flee when a predator or a diver gets close. This group includes most rays, catsharks, Tawny Nurse Shark, Leopard Shark, grubfish, gurnards, morwongs, rockcods, hawkfish, weedfish and flatheads. There is quite a crossover between these two groups, and it can be an individual thing, as some fish are naturally bold or curious, while others are shy and wary.

Photographing stationary fish is generally easy, as many will let you get close to compose your photos from the best angle. They are great subjects to practise with, allowing you to take your time, play around with lighting techniques and work on different compositions.

Moving fish are a great deal more difficult to photograph, especially for those using a compact camera. These again fall into different categories – the schoolers, the slow swimmers, the darters and the runaways.

Schooling fishes are generally easy to photograph, as being together they are confident with safety in numbers. Schools of trevally, barracuda, fusiliers, rabbitfish, stripeys, Old Wife, bream, coral snapper, batfish, parrotfish, sweetlips and bullseyes are all generally easy to approach and photograph. However, not all schoolers are so friendly, as schools of mobula rays and cownose rays are very wary of divers.

The slow swimmers are generally reef fishes that are easy to photograph, as they take their time swimming away. This group includes the pufferfish, porcupinefish, pineapplefish, catfish, shrimpfish, dottybacks, soapfish, cardinalfish, beardies, blue devils, boxfish and cowfish. Most of these fish are easy to approach and photograph, even with a compact camera, as they move slowly and even stop to investigate you. Other slow swimmers include the Whale Shark and manta rays. They may be big, but they do move slowly, and in the case of manta rays they are also curious and like to closely investigate divers.

The darters include many of the reef fish that never seem to stop moving as they explore the reef for food, mates or a hiding spot. This group includes the trumpetfish, coral trouts, basslets, tilefish, whiptails, damselfish, anemonefish, emperors, goatfish, butterflyfish, angelfish, wrasses, boarfish, surgeonfish, triggerfish and leatherjackets. To photograph these fish, patience and timing are required. With these fish it is best to watch them for a while to see if they have any swim patterns or a circuit they follow, then position yourself to take advantage of this. A fast shutter speed is needed for these fish – above 1/125th of a second – in order to freeze the action. If using a compact camera always pan with the fish and continue to pan as you press

Above: Photographing some fish is easier when they are getting cleaned, as demonstrated by this relaxed Pink Whipray (*Pateobatis fai*) being cleaned by a group of East-Australian Stripey (*Microcanthus joyceae*).

Below: Bottom-resting fish, such as the Jameson's Seaperch (*Hypoplectrodes jamesoni*), are generally easier to photograph.

Behaviour photos, such as this Spotted Wobbegong eating a Stout Moray, are more difficult to capture.

the shutter release, this will compensate for the shutter delay and mean the fish shouldn't swim out of the frame before the shutter has closed.

The runaways are the fish that flee from divers and snorkellers, making them next to impossible to photograph. This group includes many sharks, especially the whalers and hammerheads, and also pelagic fishes such as mackerel, tuna, marlin and sailfish. To get close enough to photograph many of these fishes baits are required, which is why shark feeds are popular. To approach these fishes, and fish in general, use a slow approach, slow your breathing, and avoid diving in crowds.

Finally, some tips on composition. Always shoot fish at eye level. If they are

The number one composition rule for good fish photos is to always have the fish's eye in focus, even with tricky subjects such as Swallowtail Basslet (*Serranocirrhitus latus*).

resting on the bottom get down low. Always try to frame the fish entering the frame, rather than leaving. This will engage the viewer more. Also make sure that the eye is always in focus, as this is critical to a successful image. And while portraits of fish are nice, for more dramatic pictures try to capture behaviour – fighting, mating, spawning, feeding or cleaning.

Photographing fishes is very challenging and also a lot of fun. You are bound to get a lot of bad fish photos, but hopefully some great ones too – it is just a matter of never giving up and enjoying meeting, observing and photographing a lot of different fishes.

Badu Island Moa Island
Horn Island
Prince of Wales Island **Cape York**

Duyfken Point
Albatross Bay

PACIFIC

Coral

Cape

Cape Grenville

York

Princess Charlotte Bay Cape Melville

Cape Flattery

Peninsula

Mitchell

Port Douglas

Cairns

Great

Barrier

Sea

OCEAN

Hinchinbrook Island

Reef

Magnetic Island

Townsville

Burdekin

Lake Dalrymple

Mackay

Whitsunday Group

Long Island
Warginburra Peninsula

Rockhampton

Curtis Island

Tropic of Capricorn

Hervey Bay Sandy Cape

Fraser Island

QUEENSLAND

Sunshine Coast

Brisbane

Gold Coast

Darling *Namoi*

NEW SOUTH

1
2
3
4
5
6
7
8
9
10
11
12
13
14
15
16
17
18
19
20
21
22
23
24
25
26
27
28
29
30
31
32
33
34
35
36
37
38

QUEENSLAND

With the Great Barrier Reef stretching along most of the Queensland coastline it is understandable why the Sunshine State is the most popular dive destination in Australia. The Great Barrier Reef is immense – the world's largest reef system, more than 2,300km long and comprising over 3,000 individual reefs. The reef contains more than 1,500 species of fishes, so is one of the best fishwatching areas in the country.

The Great Barrier Reef is Queensland's biggest asset and its most popular tourist attraction. However, beyond the reef there are other wonderful fishwatching spots. East of the reef are the isolated seamount reefs of the Coral Sea and at the southern end of the state are many fabulous rocky reefs, artificial reefs and shipwrecks. More than 3,180 species of fishes, both marine and freshwater, are found in Queensland.

The fish life in Queensland is mainly tropical, with most species seen in other parts of the Indo-Pacific region. Large numbers and a huge variety of small to medium-sized tropical fish populate every reef. The state is also home to a wonderful variety of sharks, rays, gropers and pelagic fishes.

South of the Tropic of Capricorn is Queensland's unique subtropical zone. The water is cooler in this zone, and is still mostly populated by tropical species. However, many temperate-water species also reside in this area, either permanently or temporarily on an annual migration. This is also the area where endemic fishes start to become more common.

Dive shops, day charter boats and liveaboard dive boats operate from the most popular tourist destinations off the east coast of Queensland, taking divers and snorkellers out to explore the reef and other sites. Most of Queensland's dive sites are only accessible by boat, but a few good shore diving and snorkelling spots are found in the south.

While avoiding the crowds is usually the best way to observe fishes, some of the best fishwatching spots, off cities such as Cairns, are where the large day boats take hundreds of people each day. In these places the fish have become accustomed to divers and snorkellers, so are easier to get close to.

1 RAINE ISLAND, FAR NORTHERN REEFS

Raine Island is one of the most remote islands of the Great Barrier Reef and also the most important Green Turtle nesting site in the world. More than 60,000 female turtles nest on the island each summer, and as such the island is a national park and visitors are not allowed ashore. Fortunately, you are allowed to dive on certain sections of the island's fringing reef, and see some of the wonderful fishes that gather here.

The island is located on the Far Northern section of the Great Barrier Reef, close to Cape York. This section of the Great Barrier Reef is rarely dived, due to its remote location. However, at the end of each year a handful of liveaboard dive boats venture north from Cairns to explore the Far Northern Reefs, which are some of the richest reefs in the world.

When I first dived Raine Island, more than 20 years ago, you could explore spectacular sites right around the island. Now much of the reef has restricted access,

Epaulette Shark (*Hemiscyllium ocellatum*).

Redstripe Basslet (*Pseudanthias fasciatus*).

so diving is limited to the eastern end of the reef. This is hardly an issue as this part of the reef has wonderful hard corals in the shallows, plus many gutters, ledges and a drop-off to explore. All of which are home to a great collection of fishes.

Tiger Sharks are attracted to Raine Island during the turtle nesting season, and pick off the weak, sick and injured. Many divers have encountered a Tiger Shark at this site and found them to be shy and wary creatures. I haven't been fortunate enough to see one yet, although I have seen plenty of other sharks there.

Grey Reef Sharks are often seen cruising the drop-off. However, they rarely come close to divers. You will have better luck getting close to the Whitetip Reef Sharks that patrol the shallows and rest in the many ledges and caves. These ledges also provide a resting spot for Ornate Wobbegongs and cute Epaulette Sharks.

Also known as walking sharks, because they walk across the bottom on their pectoral fins, Epaulette Sharks are usually only seen at night and hide under ledges by day to avoid predators. However, I saw quite a few at Raine Island that started to get active in the afternoon. These cute sharks are endemic to the Great Barrier Reef and grow to 1m long.

Spotted Porcupinefish (*Diodon hystrix*).

Common reef fishes seen at Raine Island include wrasses, parrotfish, triggerfish, surgeonfish, goatfish, coral snappers, sweetlips, angelfish, rockcods, butterflyfish and damsels. Larger fish include mackerel, trevally, batfish, barracuda, Dogtooth Tuna and a few Giant Maori Wrasse.

Splashes of colour are added on the drop-off by groups of basslets, including some very pretty Redstripe Basslets. Basslets are always fun to watch as they hover in the current and dart back and forth to feed on plankton. They live in harems, with a dominant male and his collection of female partners. If he dies one of the females changes sex and takes his place.

It is well worth investigating the many ledges that cut the reef at Raine Island. These provide shelter for many fishes, including soapfish, squirrelfish, blennies, Pacific Trumpetfish, dottybacks, boxfish, pufferfish, cardinalfish and some rather large Spotted Porcupinefish. The Spotted Porcupinefish grows to 70cm in length and feeds at night on crustaceans, molluscs and sea urchins. They are generally a little sleepy during the day, which makes it easy to closely study these spiky fish.

2 DEEP PINNACLE, GREAT DETACHED REEF, FAR NORTHERN REEFS

The remote Far Northern Reefs stretch from Lizard Island to the Torres Strait. The main body of reefs form a barrier between the Pacific Ocean and the Australian mainland. However, there are several isolated reefs beyond the main reef line that rise from the depths and offer exceptional diving. Of these, Great Detached Reef is the most famous.

There are fabulous dive sites right around Great Detached Reef, but the feature that makes this reef extra special is its deep lagoon. This lagoon is dotted with countless coral heads, or pinnacles, and each one is packed with marine life. I have dived a number of these pinnacles, with one of the best for fishwatching being Deep Pinnacle.

Rising from 60m, this pinnacle is in much deeper water than the other pinnacles in the lagoon with its twin peaks rising to 20m and 14m. As such the coral growth on the structure is spectacular, with colourful gorgonians, soft corals and sponges. And living among the corals is a great assortment of fishes. Common species include a variety of fusiliers, butterflyfish, wrasses, parrotfish, pufferfish, rockcods, lizardfish, goatfish, coral snapper, surgeonfish, triggerfish, hawkfish, sweetlips, angelfish, damsels, basslets and anemonefish.

Silvertip Sharks are always seen at Deep Pinnacle. Unfortunately, they are a little camera-shy, keeping their distance from divers. Trevally, batfish, gropers and barracuda also cruise the site.

While watching the big fish and sharks is always entertaining, the most interesting fishes at this site are small and often a little harder to find. Tiny blennies

Orange-spotted Pipefish (*Corythoichthys ocellatus*).

and threefins sit on the corals. Also, keep an eye out for Orange-spotted Pipefish. These delicate little fish only grow to 11cm in length, and their spotted pattern aids camouflage. They are often found in pairs, so if you spot one have a look around for its mate.

Make sure you investigate all the nooks and crannies at this site as you might spot a rare Striped Boxfish. The males of this species are black and blue, and the females black and yellow, and both have a pretty striped pattern. Like all boxfish they are shy, so surprising one under a ledge is often the only way to get a good look at one.

The most interesting fish I found on Deep Pinnacle was a first for me – a spectacular Barred Snakemoray. This strange-looking eel had a very impressive set of dentures, almost a mouth full of teeth, and two strange knobs on its head. I only got a brief look, and a handful of images, before this unique eel disappeared into its lair. It took me a while to identify this moray as there were no records of this species being found in Australian waters!

Above: Female Striped Boxfish (*Ostracion solorensis*).

Left: Barred Snakemoray (*Uropterygius fasciolatus*).

3 THE PINNACLE, GREAT DETACHED REEF, FAR NORTHERN REEFS

There are hundreds of sites for divers to investigate on the Far Northern Reefs and new sites are being found on each trip during exploratory dives. In this area divers can explore walls, sloping reefs, coral caves and coral gardens. However, the best sites for fishwatching are the many pinnacles, or bommies as Australians call them.

The Pinnacle is not far from Deep Pinnacle. However, rising from 40m to 4m, it is a lot shallower, so allowing more bottom time to explore and find fishes. This giant mound of coral is decorated by soft corals and gorgonians and has many ledges and overhangs to explore.

Female Swallowtail Angelfish (*Genicanthus melanospilos*).

A similar collection of reef fish are found at this site, although I also spotted more scorpionfish, including a lovely Leaf Scorpionfish. The Pinnacle also has a good collection of sea anemones populated by at least three different species of anemonefish – Pink, Clark's and Spinecheek Anemonefish. Each species lives in its own anemone, and they don't like to share with other anemonefish species, although they do share with small Threespot Humbugs.

A good variety of pretty butterflyfish and angelfish are seen on every dive at The Pinnacle. Pinstripe, Saddle, Bluespot, Blacklip and Pacific Double-saddle Butterflyfish and Blue, Bicolor, Pearlscale and Threespot Angelfish are some of the species easily found. However, I also spotted a rare angelfish at this site – the gorgeous Swallowtail Angelfish. This small angelfish grows to 18cm in length, with the male and female having completely different colour patterns – the male a striped pattern and the female a plain pattern with two bold lines on the tail.

Numerous hawkfish are seen at The Pinnacle, including the much-prized Longnose Hawkfish. These pretty fish have a lovely red-and-white chequer pattern

Longnose Hawkfish (*Oxycirrhites typus*).

Twinspot Lionfish (*Dendrochirus biocellatus*).

and an elongated snout to suck up prey. They are best found resting on gorgonian fans. However, they don't sit still for long and often lead divers on a merry chase in an attempt to photograph them.

The Pinnacle is also an excellent night dive. Sleeping fish can be found wedged into every nook and cranny, and many, like the butterflyfish, change colour at night into more drab patterns, almost like they are changing into pyjamas. Emerging at night to hunt are squirrelfish, soldierfish and lionfish. I got a big surprise at this site when I found a Twinspot Lionfish. Easily identified by the two large eye-spots on its dorsal fin, this small fish is usually very shy and not easy to find. This species is more common in Asia, and in Australia it was thought to only be found on the west coast until I spotted this one at The Pinnacle.

4 NORTH HORN, OSPREY REEF

Osprey Reef is one of the most spectacular dive destinations in the world. Located deep in the Coral Sea, 350km north-east of Cairns, the reef is the peak of an ancient mountain and covers an area of 80 sq km. Sitting in the middle of nowhere, Osprey Reef is washed by crystal-clear water, the visibility generally greater than 40m. Rising from deep water, the reef also has dramatic walls that plunge vertically 1km to the ocean floor. Add to this beautiful corals, masses of reef fish, schools of pelagic fish and a good population of sharks and it is easy to see why this destination is so highly rated.

There are several impressive dive sites at Osprey Reef, with the best for fishwatching being North Horn. Located at the northern tip of the reef, this site has been used for shark feeds for more than 30 years, so expect lots of sharks. The shark feed is action packed, and attracts dozens of Grey Reef Sharks and Whitetip Reef Sharks. However, the best time to dive the site is before the feed when the sharks and fishes are curious and closely inspect divers.

Grey Reef Sharks dominate this site, with close to 50 seen patrolling the reef and

Grey Reef Shark (*Carcharhinus amblyrhynchos*).

Clown Triggerfish (*Balistoides conspicillum*).

wall. This is usually a shy shark and hard to get close to for photos, but this is not the case at North Horn. The Grey Reef Shark grows to 2.5m in length and has a bad reputation as a territorial predator. If they feel threatened, they drop their pectoral fins and do an erratic swim display, and if ignored they have bitten divers in the past. I have encountered thousands of Grey Reef Sharks and never seen this threat display. However, I would recommend backing away quickly if you do.

Other sharks seen at North Horn including Silvertip, Tiger and Pelagic Thresher Sharks, Great Hammerhead and even Whale Shark. Schools of Scalloped Hammerheads also visit Osprey Reef during winter, although encounters are unpredictable.

Other large fishy residents of North Horn include a group of friendly Potato Cod that often get more food than the sharks at the feed. Giant Maori Wrasse, batfish, mackerel, sweetlips, trevally and barracuda are also common.

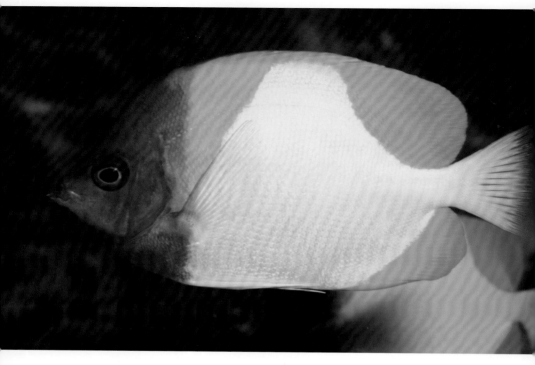

Pyramid Butterflyfish (*Hemitaurichthys polylepis*).

While the sharks and larger fish tend to get all the attention at North Horn, this site also has a good population of reef fishes. A variety of goatfish, hawkfish, surgeonfish, angelfish, damsels, wrasses, pufferfish, parrotfish and rockcods are easily spotted. This is also an excellent location to see one of the most colourful fish of the reef, the Clown Triggerfish. This multicoloured fish has a sandpaper-like skin instead of scales, and triggerfish also have a sharp dorsal spine that they can trigger erect for defence. Triggerfish also use this spine to lock themselves in place in a hole in the reef, so making it harder for a predator to dislodge them. The Clown Triggerfish grows up to 50cm in length and is mostly seen on drop-offs.

North Horn is also a good spot to see schools of Pyramid Butterflyfish. Most butterflyfish are seen in pairs and feed on coral polyps. However, Pyramid Butterflyfish feed on plankton and do this by gathering in large schools. They are generally only seen on drop-offs that are washed by currents and a constant supply of plankton, so North Horn is the perfect spot to watch them feed.

5   COD HOLE, LIZARD ISLAND

Cod Hole is one of the most famous dive sites on the Great Barrier Reef because of its resident population of large and friendly Potato Cod. Located close to Lizard Island, the friendly gropers of Cod Hole were discovered by Ron and Val Taylor in 1973. They recognised how unique the site was and fought to get it protected from anglers, finally achieving that goal in 1981. Today these gropers are some of the most watched fish in Australia.

The reef at Cod Hole is a series of ridges and gutters that slopes off into a deep channel. When first discovered, the site was home to around 25 Potato Cod. However, today that number has unfortunately dwindled to less than a dozen. A few liveaboard boats, and day boats from Lizard Island, visit the site to feed the gropers. Anywhere from two to ten Potato Cod turn up for the feed, but generally only one dominant fish gets most of the food, chasing the other gropers away.

The free food also attracts Mangrove Jacks, Two-spot Red Bass, Midnight Snapper, fusiliers and other freeloaders. While the fish feed is good fun, you actually see more fish just swimming around the reef. And once the food is gone the Potato Cod are more relaxed and easier to approach and photograph, especially if you find one enjoying the services of a Common Cleaner Wrasse.

Potato Cod (*Epinephelus tukula*).

There are actually a number of cleaning stations at Cod Hole where you can watch the busy groups of Common Cleaner Wrasse servicing their clients. Most fish, including sharks, use the services of these cleaners to remove parasites, old skin and even food stuck between their teeth. The fish queue up for the service and it is always amazing to watch one of these tiny fish gamely enter the gills and mouth of much larger fish, including fish that normally eat other fish!

Cruising the coral gardens at Cod Hole, divers will see a variety of rockcods, rabbitfish, coral snappers, morays, sweetlips, butterflyfish, coral trout, triggerfish, wrasses, boxfish, pufferfish, angelfish, anemonefish, damsels, goatfish and surgeonfish. Schools of Bumphead Parrotfish are sometimes seen in the morning, moving through the site as they graze on algae.

The deeper reef slope is the best spot to see Giant Maori Wrasse, Grey Reef Shark and Whitetip Reef Shark. If a current is present, keep an eye out for passing pelagic fish such as Rainbow Runner, mackerel, trevally and barracuda.

Cod Hole is also a good spot for small and unusual fishes. Many years ago, there use to be a small group of Bargibant's Pygmy Seahorses living on a gorgonian fan in deeper water. These cute seahorses only grow to 2cm in length and have a colour pattern and body decorations that perfectly match their host gorgonian, which makes them the masters of camouflage and very difficult to find. Other small fishes seen at this site include pipefish, blennies, shrimp gobies and Leaf Scorpionfish.

Opposite: Common Cleaner Wrasse (*Labroides dimidiatus*) cleaning the gills of a batfish.
Above: Bargibant's Pygmy Seahorse (*Hippocampus bargibanti*).

6 CHALLENGER BAY, RIBBON REEFS

The Ribbon Reefs are a string of ten elongated reefs north of Cairns that offer some of the best diving on the Great Barrier Reef. These remote reefs can only be explored from a liveaboard boat, and are dotted with dozens of fabulous dive sites that are overloaded with reef fishes.

Challenger Bay is located on Ribbon Reef No.10 and used to have beautiful coral gardens. Unfortunately, much of the coral was destroyed by a cyclone, but it is making a recovery. And while the coral is not as good as it use to be, the fish life is still impressive.

The best place to start looking for unusual fishes is on the sandy slope, beyond the coral gardens. This is a good spot to see Coral Sea Maskrays, goatfish, grubfish, shrimp gobies and the occasional flounder. However, the real prize is the large colony of Spotted Garden Eels.

These bizarre eels live their entire life in the sand, with only their head and part of their body emerging to feed on zooplankton. Living in large colonies, which can number in the hundreds, they even remain in their sandy home when mating, simply intertwining with their closest neighbour to spawn. Garden eels are best observed from a distance as they wave back and forth feeding, as any attempt to get close will see them disappear into the sand.

The coral gardens at Challenger Bay still teem with fishes. Commonly seen are parrotfish, butterflyfish, angelfish, damsels, lionfish, surgeonfish, fusiliers, triggerfish, rockcods, coral trout, pufferfish and wrasses. In the early morning herds of Bumphead Parrotfish can sometimes be seen emerging from their night-time hiding spots to have a breakfast of algae, scraped off the rocks and coral with their powerful beaks.

Also patrolling the coral gardens are Whitetip Reef Shark, Giant Maori Wrasse, trevally, mackerel and barracuda. Small groups of Oblique-banded Sweetlips hover on the coral heads to get cleaned, allowing divers to get very close for photos. These sweetlips are very common on the northern section of the Great Barrier Reef, spending the day suspended over coral heads. At night they disperse, hunting the sand for small invertebrates. When resting by day, groups of Oblique-banded Sweetlips are often joined by batfish, and on one dive I observed a Starry Puffer that thought it was part of the group.

A night dive is a very rewarding experience at Challenger Bay, as many predators

Spotted Garden Eel (*Heteroconger hassi*).

feed at this site. Patrolling overhead are Grey Reef Sharks, while more active on the bottom, searching every crack and crevice, are dozens of Whitetip Reef Sharks. They are looking for sleeping fish, and even batter themselves against the coral in their search. Hunting with them are huge Giant Trevally, Two-spot Red Bass and a few Common Lionfish.

Even more impressive are the hunting Giant Morays. Growing to 3m in length, these eels are an impressive sight when out in the open and looking for prey. They snap at any fish they disturb, and having seen one bite a fusilier in two, it is a humbling sight.

Above: Oblique-banded Sweetlips (*Plectorhinchus lineatus*).

Left: Giant Moray (*Gymnothorax javanicus*).

7 PIXIE PINNACLE, RIBBON REEFS

Pinnacles or bommies are great places to fishwatch. This is because these towers of coral are generally isolated from other reefs, becoming oases for fishes looking for food and shelter. In effect, they concentrate a whole community of fishes, that are more spread out on reefs, into a much smaller area. Pixie Pinnacle is a great example of this.

This wonderful pinnacle is located off Pixie Reef, a small reef near Ribbon Reef No.9. Rising from 35m to 4m, Pixie Pinnacle is decorated with a colourful variety of hard corals, soft corals, gorgonians, sea whips and sponges. Starting at the base of this pinnacle, first look for the bigger stuff – Whitetip Reef Shark, Blackspotted Groper and stingrays hanging around the sandy bottom.

Blackhead Leatherjacket (*Pervagor melanocephalus*).

Sea Whip Goby (*Bryaninops yongei*).

Pelagic fish constantly swing by Pixie Pinnacle hoping to pick up a quick snack. Keep an eye out for barracuda, trevally, Rainbow Runner and mackerel. A variety of batfish also visit the pinnacle, either individually or in groups.

As you circle the pinnacle, making your way back into shallow water, you will see numerous reef fishes, such as hawkfish, wrasses, butterflyfish, angelfish, surgeonfish, squirrelfish, cardinalfish, lionfish, lizardfish and damsels.

A number of leatherjackets, or filefish as they are called overseas, can be seen at this site. Australia is home to a huge variety of leatherjackets, around 58 species, most of which are found in southern waters. However, a few species are found in the tropics, and they are mostly small and easily overlooked, like the Blackhead Leatherjacket. Only growing to 10cm in length, this pretty reef fish is shy and unassuming, and darts between the corals as it looks for tiny invertebrates to eat. To get a good look at one you must be very patient.

With sea whips sprouting from the sides of this pinnacle this is a great spot to look for Sea Whip Gobies. These tiny fish are semi-transparent and only 3cm long, so not easy to spot as they cling to their sea whip home. Sea Whip Gobies, like their host, feed on plankton, so are generally seen in spots with current. And to avoid being

Masked Rabbitfish (*Siganus puellus*).

swept away they have modified pelvic fins that allow them to grip. Photographing and observing these gobies is never easy, as they like to avoid attention. The best time to observe them is when they are guarding their eggs, which naturally they lay on the sea whip.

The top of Pixie Pinnacle is alive with small fishes – anemonefish, pipefish, parrotfish, triggerfish, basslets, wrasses, blennies and a huge variety of damsels. A number of rabbitfish species are also seen. Some rabbitfish species school and others are seen in pairs, such as the Masked Rabbitfish. These lovely-looking fish dart around the reef, scraping off algae, and like all rabbitfish they have venomous spines for defence.

GORGONIAN WALL, RIBBON REEFS

Many of the famous dive sites on the Ribbon Reefs are giant coral bommies, but on Ribbon Reef No.5 is an impressive coral cliff called Gorgonian Wall. Dropping from the surface to 36m, this wall is decorated with many pretty corals and home to some very interesting fishes.

Most dives at Gorgonian Wall start on a huge bommie that sits proud of the wall. This coral head swarms with small fishes, including damsels, basslets, wrasses, butterflyfish and goatfish. Several White-banded Cleaner Shrimps have set up a cleaning station here, and if you wait patiently you can see them climb onto small fish to clean them.

From this bommie you head right to explore the main wall. Pelagic fish are commonly seen patrolling the wall, including trevally, mackerel, fusiliers and batfish. Many large gorgonians sprout from the wall, and one is reported to house a group of Bargibant's Pygmy Seahorses. Unfortunately, I couldn't find them on my last visit.

Barred Angelfish (*Paracentropyge multifasciatus*).

Yellow Scissortail (*Assessor flavissimus*).

The wall itself is cut by many nooks and crannies, and home to small reef fish such as hawkfish, boxfish, rockcods, triggerfish, pufferfish and angelfish. One special fish to look for here is the Barred Angelfish. This rarely seen small angelfish grows to 12cm in length and is very cryptic, with a preference for hiding in caves. When you do find one look around as they are often seen in pairs. However, a male can also have several females in his gang. You have to be quite patient to observe and photograph Barred Angelfish as they are very skittish.

The left section of Gorgonian Wall is also cut with many caves and recesses, with a few overhangs having sandy patches where shrimp gobies and Twinspot Goby can be found. While numerous reef fish constantly swim along the wall, I would suggest investigating the many caves for more interesting species. Here you will see squirrelfish, soldierfish, Bicoloured Dottybacks and some lovely Swallowtail Basslets. However, have a good look for tiny blue and yellow fishes – these are scissortails.

Arrowhead Soapfish (*Belonoperca chabanaudi*).

The Blue Scissortail and Yellow Scissortail are members of the longfin family, and grow to 6cm in length, although most are only 2–3cm long. The Yellow Scissortails are more attractive and photogenic, but both species are trickly to observe, as they swim underside down and are quick to dart away if a light shines on them. Scissortails are mouth brooders, with the male keeping the eggs in his mouth for around 15 days until they hatch.

A number of soapfish are also found in these caves, with the Barred Soapfish the easiest species to see. A more obscure member of this family can also be found here – the Arrowhead Soapfish. This species is nocturnal, so best seen at night. Soapfish are placed in the groper family, and have toxins in the skin that lathers like soap when released, hence the name soapfish.

9 STEVE'S BOMMIE, RIBBON REEFS

Steve's Bommie is one of the most popular dive sites on the Great Barrier Reef for one simple reason – masses of fish. Rising from 30m to 3m, the peak of this pinnacle is always swarming with fishes – schools of trevally, coral snappers, goatfish, fusiliers, surgeonfish and barracuda. There can be so many fishes that divers can easily lose sight of their dive buddy!

Watching all these fishes can be mesmerising. However, you will miss out on this bommie's other fish treats if you stay in the shallows. At the base of the bommie are some lovely corals and sponges, and this is the best place to see Spotted Eagle Ray, Coral Sea Maskray, Giant Maori Wrasse, Whitetip Reef Shark and a number of gropers.

As you explore Steve's Bommie you will see a wide variety of wrasses, rockcods, basslets, butterflyfish, angelfish, rabbitfish, surgeonfish, damsels, goatfish, parrotfish, hawkfish, cardinalfish and pufferfish. Numerous ledges and crevices cut the bommie, most sheltering reef fish and the occasional Ornate Wobbegong.

Orangestripe Triggerfish (*Balistapus undulatus*).

Reef Stonefish (*Synanceia verrucosa*).

One of the most colourful fish sheltering in these recesses are Orangestripe Triggerfish. These pretty patterned fish are always seen sneaking in and out of their hideouts as they are shy of divers. However, they are very territorial with other fishes. They have very strong teeth and feed on a range of prey, including molluscs, crustaceans and echinoderms. Orangestripe Triggerfish are thought to perform a very important role in keeping sea urchin numbers in check by eating them.

Scorpionfishes are over-represented on Steve's Bommie, so always watch where you put your hands. Look for lionfish, Leaf Scorpionfish and Raggy Scorpionfish. Even the elusive and rare Lacy Scorpionfish has also been seen at this site. Far more common, and well hidden, is a population of Reef Stonefish.

Not the prettiest of fish, even though some of the ones seen here are very colourful, the Reef Stonefish is highly venomous with 13 lethal spines on the dorsal fin. At Steve's Bommie they hide among the coral, bury in the rubble or tuck up

Eastern Clown Anemonefish (*Amphiprion percula*).

under ledges. However, on one memorable dive I watched five of them chasing each other across the reef in what may have been a mating ritual.

On the top of Steve's Bommie, have a look for small fishes among the corals. This is a good spot to see pipefish, blennies, tobies, threefins and juvenile boxfish. There is also a group of Eastern Clown Anemonefish in one anemone that are very photogenic.

Made popular in the film *Finding Nemo*, Eastern Clown Anemonefish are always popular with divers and great fun to watch. Like other anemonefish, the largest fish in the group is the female and the second-largest is her male partner. The other smaller fish in the group are not their kids, but other small males. If the female dies, her male partner changes sex and becomes the dominant female and one of the smaller males grows to become her partner. In the film Nemo's mum dies, although they didn't quite follow the script and have his dad become his mum!

10 BARRACUDA BOMMIE, AGINCOURT REEFS, PORT DOUGLAS

The Agincourt Reefs is a complex of four reefs off Port Douglas that is popular with day boats. There are dozens of wonderful dives sites at the reefs, with divers able to explore coral gardens, walls and pinnacles. Barracuda Bommie is located at the top end of Agincourt Reef No.2 and is a great spot for fishwatching.

This coral tower rises from 26m to almost touch the surface. At the base of the bommie is a sandy plain dotted with several small coral heads, which is the best place to start your dive. These coral heads are home to a variety of cardinalfish, fusiliers, damsels, anemonefish and wrasses. Numerous rockcods can also be seen. These small gropers are generally observed resting on the bottom, watching the world go by or looking for potential prey.

The most common species seen here is Coral Rockcod, but look also for Blacktip, Birdwire and Highfin Rockcods. My favourite is the Flagtail Rockcod, which has a

Spotted Sweetlips (*Plectorhinchus chaetodonoides*).

Flagtail Rockcod (*Cephalopholis urodeta*).

white V-shaped pattern on its tail. A shy species, and quite small, only growing to 28cm in length, the best time to observe Flagtails is when they are preoccupied when getting cleaned.

Also look around the sand as a colony of Spotted Garden Eels lives here. The sand is also a good spot to see grubfish, goatfish and a few shrimp gobies. Coral Sea Maskrays like to dig in this area looking for food. Until recently this species was thought to be the widespread Bluespotted Maskray, but DNA studies showed that populations were actually six separate regional species. Only found on the Great Barrier Reef, the Coral Sea Maskray differs from the other species visually in having smaller blue spots.

Like all bommies, the best way to explore Barracuda Bommie is by slowly circumnavigating the structure. As you do so you will see a good variety of small to medium-sized reef fishes. Look for schools of coral snapper, batfish, surgeonfish, fusiliers, triggerfish and unicornfish.

Several sweetlips call this bommie home, including a few Spotted Sweetlips. Most sweetlips hang out in small groups, but Spotted Sweetlips seem to like their own company and are usually seen alone hovering under ledges.

Coral Sea Maskray (*Neotrygon trigonoides*).

Pelagic fish also gather at Barracuda Bommie, with trevally, mackerel and naturally, as the name of the site suggests, barracuda. Also keep an eye out for Snubnose Dart as I have seen a few at this spot.

You can either end your dive on top of the bommie, looking at all the small fishes, or swim over to the adjacent reef, which has lovely hard-coral gardens. Either way you are likely to see butterflyfish, angelfish, wrasses, parrotfish and a great variety of damsels.

11 CASTLE ROCK, AGINCOURT REEFS, PORT DOUGLAS

Castle Rock is one of the most popular dive sites on the Agincourt Reefs, as it has some wonderful coral gardens, a large bommie and is a great place to fishwatch. This is a site popular with both divers and snorkellers, with divers going deeper to explore the bommie and snorkellers hanging around the coral gardens.

Divers exploring the bommie are bound to meet Colin, the resident Blackspotted Groper. This friendly groper will generally greet divers on their way to the bottom. He is so accustomed to divers that you will have no trouble getting a close photo;

Blackspotted Groper (*Epinephelus malabaricus*).

the problem may be him being too close though, sticking his nose on your camera lens. Colin is just over a metre long, so he has a lot of growing to do, as Blackspotted Gropers can grow to more than 2m in length.

He is not the only member of the groper family seen at Castle Rock, as divers will also see Flowery, Greasy, Blacklip and Birdwire Rockcods. The main bommie at Castle Rock doesn't have the best coral coverage, although it still attracts a good variety of fish. Schools of coral snapper, fusiliers and basslets are common, also seen are sweetlips, damsels, goatfish, wrasses, surgeonfish, squirrelfish and rabbitfish.

Darting between the corals at this site are always a few Birdnose Wrasse. These strange-looking fish have an elongated snout, which they use to pick crabs, shrimps and brittle stars out of hiding spots in the coral. Like many wrasse, the males, females and juveniles all have different colour patterns – the males green, the females black and white, and the juveniles similar to the females except with two black stripes. Watching and photographing Birdnose Wrasse is always challenging as they never stop moving, darting among the corals looking for a snack.

The prettiest part of Castle Rock is the coral gardens in the shallows. Look here for lionfish, damsels, parrotfish, anemonefish, Moorish Idols and a good collection of butterflyfish. There is usually a school of Blue-lined Coral Snappers milling around the hard corals.

Birdnose Wrasse (*Gomphosus varius*).

Regal Angelfish (*Pygoplites diacanthus*).

Quite a few angelfish are found at Castle Rock, including small Coral Beauties and Bicolor Angelfish and larger Sixband Angelfish. My favourites at Castle Rock are the spectacular Regal Angelfish. One the prettiest of all the angelfish, and that is saying something as angelfish are the beauty-queens of the fish world, the Regal Angelfish is generally found in pairs or small groups. They feed mainly on sponges and tunicates and are often found in caves picking at the ceiling for a tasty treat.

12 TROPPOS, NORMAN REEF, CAIRNS

airns is a destination that many divers avoid in the belief that the large volume of visitors on day boats has destroyed its reefs. Nothing could be further from the truth, as the great majority of visitors to Cairns are snorkellers who mostly float on the surface. Also, all the guides take great pride in the reef and its inhabitants, so fully brief visitors to look and don't touch.

There are so many great dive sites off Cairns that are perfect for fishwatching that I had to limit my selection to just three. Norman Reef is the northernmost reef dived from Cairns, and as an outer reef it is washed with clear water and home to an abundance of fishes.

Red Firegoby (*Nemateleotris magnifica*).

Girdled Cardinalfish (*Taeniamia zosterophora*).

There are several brilliant dive sites at Norman Reef, with Troppos, at its northern tip, a favourite for fishwatching. This site has coral gardens in the shallows that are prefect for snorkelling and also walls, bommies and an interesting sandy slope that divers will enjoy.

I like to start on the sandy slope, as this is a great place to see unusual fishes. Look for shrimp gobies, glider gobies, Coral Sea Maskrays, grubfish and if you are lucky you might even see a Flagtail Blanquillo. This shy and elusive member of the tilefish family will disappear into a hole in the sand when a diver gets too close. Far more common at Troppos is another elusive species, the Whitepatch Razorfish.

This strange member of the wrasse family lives only in sandy areas, and dives into the sand when it feels threatened. Whitepatch Razorfish grow to 24cm in length and are very thin-bodied, which gives them their name, and also allows them to quickly burrow into the sand. This is a hard species to get close too and it is always best observed from a distance.

The coral gardens at Troppos are home to a great assortment of reef fishes,

Whitepatch Razorfish (*Iniistius aneitensis*).

including a variety of parrotfish, wrasses, angelfish, butterflyfish, goatfish, rockcods, surgeonfish, pufferfish and damsels. Batfish, Giant Maori Wrasse, Whitetip Reef Shark and trevally are also seen at the site.

In the gutters between coral heads you might see a few Red Firegobies. These lovely fish grow to 9cm long and are generally seen in pairs or in small groups of juveniles. They live in burrows in the rubble and are quick to retreat into their home at the first sign of danger. Red Firegobies are a type of dartfish and feed on zooplankton.

Sheltering in the hard corals at Troppos are numerous damsels and cardinalfish, including groups of Girdled Cardinalfish. These tiny fish only grow to 8cm in length and have a semi-transparent body; they look plain and unassuming, but at night they attract small prey with their bioluminescent bodies. This form of cold lighting is used by many sea creatures to either attract prey or a mate, or to deter predators.

13 TWIN PEAKS, SAXON REEF, CAIRNS

Saxon Reef is located north of Cairns and is a small outer reef with several wonderful dive sites. My favourite is Twin Peaks, off the south-west corner of the reef.

Two large coral bommies dominate this site, rising from 22m to just below the surface. The best place to start looking for fishes is on the sand, as here you will see Coral Sea Maskray, Bluespotted Feathertail Stingray, grubfish, goatfish and gobies. While glider gobies, sand gobies and shrimp gobies can all be seen, I like to look for the more colourful Old Glory Goby. These pretty fish grow to 8cm in length and live in holes in the sand. I am not sure how they got that strange name – I prefer their other common name of Court Jester Goby, which more suits their lovely colour patterns.

Small seaweeds sprout from the sand and provide a home for some very unusual fishes. Keen-eyed divers have spotted Hairy Ghostpipefish, Coleman's Pygmy Seahorse and several species of pipefish. However, the very strange Little Dragonfish, a type of seamoth, has also been spotted. These bizarre fish look like an insect, and crawl across the bottom on modified fins eating small invertebrates. They are often found in pairs, and when mating perform a ritualised dance before releasing their eggs and sperm.

Old Glory Goby (*Amblygobius rainfordi*).

Juvenile Spotted Parrotfish (*Cetoscarus ocellatus*).

Exploring the bommies and the nearby coral gardens, divers will see a great collection of reef fishes. Commonly encountered are various species of anemonefish, butterflyfish, angelfish, pufferfish, goatfish, parrotfish, rockcod, surgeonfish, wrasse, rabbitfish and tuskfish. Hiding in the coral are also hawkfish, blennies, threefins, coral gobies and a good assortment of damsels. However, I have also seen some wonderful juvenile fish at Twin Peaks, including small boxfish, wrasses and sweetlips.

Over the years I have observed several juvenile Spotted Parrotfish roaming the corals at Twin Peaks. Like all parrotfish, this species has different colour patterns for males, females and juveniles; they are so different that you would think they are different species. The bold white-and-orange pattern of the juvenile Spotted Parrotfish makes them quite conspicuous, although they are never easy to get close to. Parrotfish graze on algae, which they scrape off corals and rocks, with a by-product of this being sand. It is thought that they poo so much sand that most tropical beaches are made of parrotfish poo!

Larger fish seen at Twin Peaks including groups of Oblique-banded Sweetlips, Giant Maori Wrasse, Whitetip Reef Shark, gropers, batfish, trevally and mackerel.

Little Dragonfish (*Eurypegasus draconis*).

14 OASIS, MILLN REEF, CAIRNS

Milln Reef is another outer reef with several fabulous dive sites. My pick of the sites is Oasis, as the varied terrain of coral gardens in the shallows and bommies in deeper water means there is always a wonderful variety of fishes.

This is a site where it is easy to get lost as the bommies in deeper water form a maze. However, this is the best place to see pelagic fish and sharks. Whitetip Reef Sharks and Grey Reef Sharks patrol this area, while schools of trevally, batfish and barracuda swim between the bommies. Schools of Blackfin and Pickhandle Barracuda are common, and Great Barracuda also visit this reef.

The largest member of the family, the Great Barracuda can grow to 2m in length. They have a reputation as being dangerous, attacking shiny objects on swimmers and divers. This is because they are opportunistic feeders that launch rapid attacks to grab sick, weak or injured fish. I have never found them to be aggressive. At Oasis

Great Barracuda (*Sphyraena barracuda*) being cleaned by a Bicolor Cleanerfish (*Labroides bicolor*).

Raggy Scorpionfish (*Scorpaenopsis venosa*).

I was fortunate to watch one getting cleaned by a Bicolor Cleaner Wrasse. This barracuda was so relaxed and enjoying this service that I was able to get very close to watch the process and get some photos.

These bommies are also a great spot to see schools of coral snapper, rabbitfish, surgeonfish, fusiliers and basslets. While exploring the coral gardens look for stingrays, damsels, goatfish, Moorish Idols, butterflyfish, angelfish, pufferfish, boxfish and wrasses. I have also seen a few scorpionfish resting on the corals at Oasis, including the most common reef species, the Raggy Scorpionfish.

Like all scorpionfish this species has venomous spines, and believe me you don't want to be jabbed by any member of this family as it hurts like hell. The Raggy Scorpionfish is easily confused with several similar-looking scorpionfish seen on the Great Barrier Reef, as they all have a mottled pattern and fleshy filaments across the body and around the mouth to form a beard.

Titan Triggerfish (*Balistoides viridescens*).

One potentially dangerous fish to watch for at Oasis is the Titan Triggerfish. Most triggerfish are small, shy and unassuming, but not so the Titan Triggerfish. This species grows to 75cm in length and has large stumpy teeth. They use these teeth to break open urchins, molluscs and crustaceans, and also to move pieces of coral when looking for food. Titan Triggerfish are usually observed going about their daily lives and mostly ignore divers, except when nesting. Then they get extremely defensive and territorial. The female digs a nest in the sand or coral rubble to lay her eggs, and attacks any fish or diver that gets close to her nest. I have been chased by numerous Titan Triggerfish over the years, and fortunately never bitten. However, other divers have received very nasty bites, some requiring stitches!

15 WHEELER REEF, TOWNSVILLE

Offshore from Townsville is a great collection of coral reefs visited by day boats and liveaboard dive boats. Wheeler Reef is a small inner reef with a wonderful variety of fishes.

The western side of the reef offers the best diving, with coral gardens in the shallows and numerous bommies in deeper water. These bommies rise from 30m and are the best place to start looking for fishes. Schools of fish swarm this area, including numerous fusiliers, coral snapper, surgeonfish and trevally. A vast school of Blackfin Barracuda can sweep in and engulf divers. Also visiting these bommies are Whitetip Reef Shark, Giant Maori Wrasse, coral trout and gropers.

A closer inspection of the bommies will reveal many small reef fishes, such as angelfish, damsels, hawkfish, pufferfish and even pipefish. A number of anemonefish

Pink Anemonefish (*Amphiprion perideraion*) male tending eggs.

Blacktail Grubfish (*Parapercis queenslandica*).

populate the sea anemones that sprout between the corals, with the Pink Anemonefish the most common species. Like all anemonefish they live in groups with a large dominant female, her male partner and several smaller males. The male partner has a very important job, as he looks after the eggs. These are generally laid on a rock under or next to the anemone, so have a close look and watch the male closely. He will tend the eggs every few minutes, blowing on them to provide oxygen and picking off rubbish or removing eggs that have gone bad.

On the sand patches between these bommies look for Coral Sea Maskrays, goatfish and small gobies. There is also a colony of Spotted Garden Eels to entertain. A common species seen feeding in the sand is the Blacktail Grubfish. This species is found throughout Queensland and grows to 25cm in length. A member of the sand

Pinstripe Butterflyfish (*Chaetodon lunulatus*).

perch family, grubfish feed on invertebrates and spend most of their time resting on the sand or searching for food. They are an easy species to approach to observe and photograph, and if you want to make a new friend start digging in the sand with your fingers and the grubfish will approach to see if you uncover any tasty morsels.

Moving into the shallows at Wheeler Reef, divers and snorkellers can explore pretty hard-coral gardens. Common residents include wrasses, damsels, parrotfish, morays, goatfish, surgeonfish, tuskfish, rabbitfish and scorpionfish. Several lovely Pinstripe Butterflyfish wander these coral gardens in pairs. This widespread species is common throughout tropical Australia and grows to 15cm in length. They feed exclusively on coral polyps, and spend a great deal of their time picking at corals to extract a meal.

16 VIPER REEF LAGOON, TOWNSVILLE

One of the outer reefs off Townsville, Viper Reef is rarely visited by most dive boats. However, if conditions are calm this is a great place to dive and marvel at the fishes. While lovely coral gardens and bommies are found on the edge of this reef, my favourite spot for fishwatching is in the calm waters of the Viper Reef Lagoon.

This sandy lagoon is dotted with coral heads in depths from 16m to 2m, and has some very healthy hard corals. Swimming between the coral heads you will spot Grey Reef Shark, Whitetip Reef Shark, Giant Maori Wrasse, batfish and a few pelagic fish. The sandy bottom is also a good spot to see grubfish, goatfish and shrimp gobies.

Digging in the sand, or hiding under coral ledges, are a few Bluespotted Feathertail Rays. This small stingray species is often confused with several bluespotted maskray species, but has a distinctive oval-shaped disc and much more vivid blue spots. A shy

Bluespotted Feathertail Ray (*Taeniura lymma*).

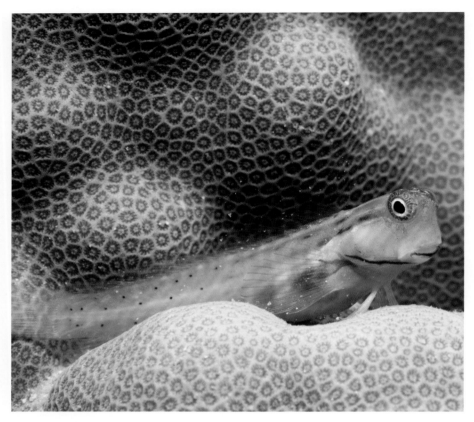

Smallspotted Combtooth Blenny (*Ecsenius stictus*).

species, they are not easy to approach or photograph, unless resting under a ledge. Like other stingray species they give birth to live young, with litters of up to seven.

Investigating the many coral heads in the lagoon, divers will see a great variety of damsels, pufferfish, surgeonfish, wrasses, rockcods, butterflyfish, cardinalfish, parrotfish and gobies. A close inspection of the corals will often reveal tiny blennies, with the Smallspotted Combtooth Blenny a common species. Also called the Great Barrier Reef Combtooth Blenny, as it is the most widespread and abundant species on the reef, this tiny fish only grows to 6cm in length. As the name suggests, combtooth blennies have comb-like teeth and feed on algae. Smallspotted Combtooth often sit on coral outcrops, so are easy to find if you stop and take your time to have a good look around a coral head.

Longtail Dottyback (*Oxycercichthys veliferus*).

In the shallows are numerous ledges and caves that are home to squirrelfish, soldierfish, cardinalfish and small angelfish. If lucky you may even spot a Longtail Dottyback. Dottybacks are secretive little fish that are easily overlooked, as they spend much of their time hiding in small hollows. They are only found in the Indo-Pacific region, and Australia is home to around 30 species. Most dottybacks are very colourful, although the Longtail Dottyback has a more subdued colouration. If you find one, stop and watch it for a while as they are quite territorial, chasing off other fish that come close to their home.

Viper Reef Lagoon is also an excellent night dive, as several Epaulette Sharks emerge from their daytime hiding spots to hunt crustaceans.

17 SS *YONGALA*, TOWNSVILLE

The SS *Yongala* is often listed in the top ten dive sites in the world, and for very good reason. This coastal steamer tragically sunk in 1911 with the loss of 123 people and is today listed as a historic shipwreck. While the 109m-long ship makes for a fascinating dive, it is the volume and variety of fishes that make this such a special dive site.

The SS *Yongala* rests in 30m of water, and being the only object in a sandy desert it acts like an oasis, attracting every fish in the area. Masses of pelagic fish swarm around the ship, including barracuda, trevally, mackerel, queenfish, bonito, Rainbow Runner and Cobia. They circle the wreck and constantly attack the smaller fishes. Joining them in this parade of fishes are Giant Maori Wrasse, Queensland Groper and schools of batfish, coral snappers, sweetlips and fusiliers.

Sharks and rays are always seen on the SS *Yongala*, with Bull Shark, Blotched Fantail Stingray, Pink Whipray, Whitespotted Wedgefish and Spotted Eagle Ray the most common species. Resting under the wreck, and sometimes inside it, are Tawny Nurse Sharks. These large reef sharks can grow to 3.2m in length and are quite docile. They have small teeth and feed on a range of prey, most of which they

Tawny Nurse Shark (*Nebrius ferrugineus*).

Barcheek Coral Trout (*Plectropomus maculatus*).

extract from the coral or sand with a powerful sucking motion. They pose no threat to divers, unless you disturb their daytime slumber and they head off in a blinding rush to escape, barrelling over a diver who gets in the way.

A number of rare rays turn up on the SS *Yongala* from time to time, including Porcupine Ray, Bowmouth Wedgefish and even the largest stingray species in the world – the Smalleye Stingray.

The wreck itself buzzes with small fishes, including dense schools of glassfish, cardinalfish and damsels. Common reef fishes include rockcods, wrasses, angelfish, hawkfish, blennies, parrotfish, goatfish, butterflyfish, surgeonfish, pufferfish and rabbitfish. Many coral trout are seen on the wreck, including both Common Coral Trout and Barcheek Coral Trout. These two species look very similar, both having blue spots, but the Barcheek has elongated spots on its head. Both are popular with fishers but fortunately, with the SS *Yongala* protected as a marine sanctuary, they are safe here.

Greenfin Parrotfish (*Chlorurus spilurus*) at night in a mucus sleeping bag.

At night the SS *Yongala* is very creepy, especially knowing it is a grave for 123 people. However, it is worth getting over any fears in order to see the nocturnal fish action. At night packs of Giant Trevally hunt, grabbing fish that haven't found a sleeping spot. They often use the torchlight of divers to locate fish, so watch where you point your torch. Also out on the hunt are Giant Morays.

Every nook and cranny on this wreck is occupied by sleeping fish, and if lucky you may even find a parrotfish tucked up in a sleeping bag. At night some parrotfish secrete a mucus cocoon from their mouth, that forms a shroud around their body. This mucus sleeping bag is thought to make it harder for predators to sniff them out, and if breached acts as an early-warning signal to allow the parrotfish to flee.

18 NORTHERN BOMMIES, MARION REEF

The Coral Sea Reefs, beyond the Great Barrier Reef, offer some of the most action-packed diving on the planet. The only problem is getting to these remote reefs, as they can only be reached by a liveaboard vessel, since most are 250km to 500km offshore. Osprey Reef is the only one of these reefs that is regularly visited. However, the others are explored from time to time on special trips. One of the least dived is Marion Reef, 400km east of the Whitsunday Coast.

Due to the lack of regular diving, no well-known dive sites exist, with each vessel simply finding its own sites. Fortunately, you can jump in just about anywhere at Marion Reef and have a great dive. When I dived this Coral Sea reef, my favourite fishwatching spot was an area we called the Northern Bommies.

The site is a series of coral ridges, gutters and bommies that are packed with fish life in depths between 10m and 30m. Sharks are common here, with a good population of Grey Reef Sharks and Whitetip Reef Sharks. Also expect to see a variety of pelagic fishes, including batfish, mackerel, Rainbow Runner, jobfish, trevally and Dogtooth Tuna. We even found one bommie that had a whirlpool of hundreds of Blackfin Barracuda circling above it.

Twospot Lizardfish (*Synodus binotatus*).

Blackaxil Puller (*Chromis atripectoralis*).

Exploring the bommies you will see a respectable variety of small and large reef fishes, such as butterflyfish, bannerfish, angelfish, parrotfish, surgeonfish, triggerfish and wrasses. Schools of coral snapper, fusiliers and goatfish hover over many of the bommies. Perched on the top of these bommies is often Twospot Lizardfish. These rather docile-looking fish are nearly always seen resting on the bottom, but don't let their lazy looks fool you as they are lethal predators. Lizardfish have a mouthful of very sharp teeth, and are ambush predators, suddenly exploding off the bottom to grab small fish and swallow them whole!

At sites like this it is tempting to leap from bommie to bommie looking for larger fishes. And I did do this on a few dives to see gropers, Tawny Nurse Sharks and a Blotched Fantail Stingray. However, to appreciate the small fish, and give them time to get used to your presence, it is nice to rest at one spot for a while. After a few minutes sitting quietly (as quietly as you can when blowing bubbles), numerous fishes emerge and go about their daily routines. I particularly like to see all the Blackaxil Pullers, a type of damsel, rising from their hiding spots among the hard corals.

Finally, a close inspection between the corals will reveal many surprises, such as blennies, tobies, gobies, threefins and hawkfish. I was delighted to find a rare Morrison's Dragonet creeping between the corals. Only 5cm long, this colourful little fish was fascinating to watch as it stopped every few seconds to grab a morsel of food. Dragonets are strange little fish as they lack scales, instead having a slimy mucous skin-covering that gives off a strong odour, leading to their other common name of stinkfish!

Morrison's Dragonet (*Neosynchiropus morrisoni*).

19 STEPPING STONES, BAIT REEF, WHITSUNDAYS

The Whitsunday Islands have some lovely dive sites, and unfortunately poor visibility. The best diving and snorkelling in this area is on the offshore reefs, with Bait Reef a popular spot for day boats and liveaboards. All around Bait Reef are wonderful dive sites, with the best spot for fishwatching a series of bommies called Stepping Stones.

Located on the sheltered western side of Bait Reef, Steeping Stones is a string of 18 large coral bommies that rise from depths between 15m and 25m and terminate just below the surface. Pretty hard corals decorate the tops of these bommies, while the caves and canyons between each are lined with gorgonians, soft corals, sponges and sea whips.

Stepping Stones is home to the usual variety of reef fishes, although it is best known for the larger fish that reside in the area. This is a great place to see one of the characters of the reef, the Giant Maori Wrasse. The largest member of the wrasse family, growing to 2.3m in length, these wonderful fish have decorative patterns on their head that look like Maori facial tattoos. Giant Maori Wrasse live for around 30

Giant Maori Wrasse (*Cheilinus undulatus*).

Flowery Rockcod (*Epinephelus fuscoguttatus*).

years, and like other wrasse are protogynous hermaphrodites, starting life as female and changing sex to male at six years of age. You can tell the difference between the sexes easily, as the males develop a large hump on their head. Giant Maori Wrasse are usually observed alone or in a male-and-female pair, However, occasionally a male will be seen with a small group of females.

Other large fish to look for include Barramundi Rockcod, Two-spot Red Bass, sweetlips, batfish, tuskfish, coral trout and parrotfish. On the deeper bommies pelagic fish are commonly seen, including trevally, barracuda, mackerel and bonito. These deeper bommies are also patrolled by Grey Reef Sharks.

Exploring the canyons and caves between the bommies, divers will also find a good population of Flowery Rockcod. These medium-sized gropers are often hard to spot, even though they grow to 1.2m in length, as they sit on the bottom and their camouflaged skin pattern helps them blend into the background. They use this

Blackspotted Pufferfish (*Arothron nigropunctatus*).

camouflage to ambush prey, grabbing any fish, crustacean or cephalopod that swims by. Flowery Rockcod also have rather large bug-eyes, possibly to assist in spotting approaching prey.

The inner side of Steeping Stones has pretty coral gardens, dominated by staghorn corals where you will see butterflyfish, angelfish, damsels and a few pufferfish. This is a good spot to see one of the fattest members of the pufferfish family, the Blackspotted Pufferfish. This species grows to 30cm in length, and like all pufferfish, it can inflate itself by gulping seawater to appear bigger and deter predators. As they get older, the Blackspotted Pufferfish seems to develop quite a large fat stomach that hangs down and wobbles around as they swim!

20 HERON BOMMIE, HERON ISLAND

Heron Island has been a popular holiday destination since the 1930s, being one of the few resorts located on a coral cay in the heart of the Great Barrier Reef. Around the island are dozens of wonderful snorkelling and diving spots, with its most famous dive site one of the best for fishwatching, Heron Bommie.

This site consists of a group of six bommies on a sandy slope in depths from 8m to 18m. Pretty gorgonians, sponges and soft corals decorate these bommies, and many turtles use this site as a place to sleep. The bommies are actually a giant cleaning station, so many fishes visit to get their daily preen.

Commonly seen around the bommies are schools of sweetlips, trevally, fusiliers, surgeonfish and coral snappers. Of the coral snappers, Hussars are the most abundant, swarming in their hundreds. These rosy-pink fish are found throughout Queensland, with Heron Island one of the few places they are seen in vast schools.

Hussar (*Lutjanus adetii*).

Coral Rockcod (*Cephalopholis miniata*).

They feed at night, dispersing over the reef to consume small fish and invertebrates. Another pretty coral snapper seen here is the Red Emperor Snapper.

Also regularly seen at Heron Bommie are gropers, stingrays, Barramundi Rockcod, Whitetip Reef Shark, Spotted Eagle Ray and barracuda. Reef Manta Rays visit these bommies to get cleaned, and are mostly seen during the winter months.

These bommie are cut with many ledges and crevices, which are a good spot for Tasselled Wobbegongs to rest. Also found in these darker recesses are squirrelfish, tuskfish, morays and a few Dusky Batfish. These large batfish grow to 45cm in length and are a key species on the Great Barrier Reef, because they eat seaweed and algae. Recent studies have shown they eat algae and seaweed that other herbivorous fish won't touch, in the process stopping the hard corals from becoming smothered. They are also a very pretty fish to watch.

A good variety of reef fish populate Heron Bommie, including angelfish, butterflyfish, wrasses, damsels, goatfish and lionfish. One thing that has always impressed me about this site is the number of Coral Rockcods. One of the loveliest

Dusky Batfish (*Platax pinnatus*).

of all the rockcods due to their polka-dot pattern, this species grows to 50cm in length, and males have a harem of females that can number up to a dozen. These fish like to hide in the nooks and crannies. However, if you wait around one of the cleaning stations you will often see them emerge to get worked over by a Common Cleaner Wrasse.

21 HERON ISLAND HARBOUR, HERON ISLAND

The harbour at Heron Island was created many years ago by cutting through the reef flat. It allows boat access to the island, but the sandy, silty bottom is easily stirred and makes visibility less than ideal compared to nearby reefs. On the upside, it has created the perfect habitat for rays and other fishes.

Snorkelling in the harbour is restricted to the early morning and late afternoon due to boat traffic. Under the jetty are always mixed schools of sweetlips, rabbitfish and surgeonfish. And swimming among them are always a few Goldspotted Groper. The sandy bottom under the jetty is a good spot to see goatfish, flounder and grubfish. However, it is the rays that most impress. Gathering here are large numbers of Pink Whiprays and Broad Cowtail Stingrays, and also a few Giant Guitarfish.

Heron Island is actually the best place in Australia to see Giant Guitarfish. This species grows to 2.7m in length, and some very large individuals can be seen here. Juveniles are also seen patrolling the shoreline at Heron Island. A type of shovelnose

Giant Guitarfish (*Glaucostegus typus*).

Porcupine Ray (*Urogymnus asperrimus*).

ray, which contains four similar-looking families, these rays are often mistaken for sharks. However, they are a ray, and like all rays they have their pectoral fins fused with the head and their gills on the underside.

Spotted Eagle Rays cruise the harbour, and Blotched Fantail Stingrays and Coral Sea Maskrays also feed here. Another rare ray seen in Heron Island Harbour is the strange Porcupine Ray. A member of the stingray family, this bizarre ray is covered in thorns and is the only stingray without a tail barb for defence. I have only seen a small number of these rays over the years, and nearly always see one on a trip to Heron Island.

Small caves and ledges line the edge of the harbour, and these are good places to see Tasselled Wobbegongs. Swimming to the harbour entrance, where the *Protector* wreck acts as a breakwater, you can also see a good variety of reef fishes such as coral snapper, surgeonfish, parrotfish, butterflyfish, wrasses and pufferfish. You are also

Whitespotted Blenny (*Salarias alboguttatus*).

likely to encounter Whitetip and Blacktip Reef Sharks cruising about in this area.

I also like to explore the shallow coral gardens each side of the harbour, as these are home to many small fishes. Expect to see pipefish, coral gobies, glider gobies, damsels, dottybacks, scissortails, threefins and a good variety of blennies. I have seen Lined Fangblenny, Queensland Combtooth Blenny and numerous Banded Blennies here. My favourites are the Whitespotted Blennies that pop out of holes all over the place. On one memorable snorkel I was watching a small Green Turtle getting cleaned by surgeonfish when I noticed a Whitespotted Blenny sitting on its shell. I'm not sure why it was sitting there – probably it was doing a little cleaning of its own.

22 ENTRANCE BOMMIE, LADY MUSGRAVE ISLAND

The Capricorn and Bunker Group is a wonderful collection of reefs and coral cays at the southern end of the Great Barrier Reef. Heron Island and Lady Elliot Island are the two most famous islands of this group, with resorts for extended stays. However, if you only have time for a day trip in this region, then Lady Musgrave Island is the spot for you.

Day boats depart from Bundaberg to explore Lady Musgrave Island, which has a large sheltered lagoon for snorkellers and a fringing reef for divers. A dozen great dive sites are found around the reef, with my favourite for fishes being Entrance Bommie.

Located near the channel that gives access to the lagoon, Entrance Bommie is not a towering pinnacle, but a large coral ridge sitting in 23m of water. This ridge is cut with many ledges and caves, so a great habitat for a range of fishes. Spend some time investigating these ledges and caves, as many are filled with schools of glassfish and sweepers. At times you have to part these small fishes like a curtain to see what else is hidden in these dark recesses. I have encountered squirrelfish,

Tasselled Wobbegong (*Eucrossorhinus dasypogon*).

Juvenile Barramundi Rockcod (*Chromileptes altivelis*).

angelfish, soapfish, morays, dottybacks and gropers.

I have also been fortunate to observe Tawny Nurse Sharks and Tasselled Wobbegongs sheltering in these caves. The Tasselled Wobbegong is a tropical species that is also found in Papua New Guinea and eastern Indonesia. They have the best camouflage of any wobbegong, and I have placed my hand on several while taking photos, thinking it was a rock! The Tasselled Wobbegong is an ambush predator, and has a trick up its sleeve to attract prey, as its tail is shaped like a fish, even having an eye-spot. It flicks and weaves its tail near its mouth hoping that a curious fish will come and investigate.

Entrance Bommie is also a great spot to see Whitetip Reef Shark, Spotted Eagle

Juvenile Yellow Boxfish (*Ostracion cubicus*).

Ray and several stingray species. The coral gardens on the top of the ridge host a range of reef fish, including a few juveniles. I have seen juvenile angelfish, sweetlips and wrasses, but the most attractive are the juvenile Yellow Boxfish and Barramundi Rockcod. Both these species like to hide among the coral, although they behave very differently.

The Yellow Boxfish darts about, and if you follow one with your camera, they often turn around to see what is trailing them, allowing for a few quick photos. By contrast the Barramundi Rockcod likes to dance with its head down and flailing its long fins about. It generally doesn't move much, although it is still a challenging fish to photograph as it twists and turns doing its dance.

23 THE BLOWHOLE, LADY ELLIOT ISLAND

Lady Elliot Island is the southernmost reef on the Great Barrier Reef and the site of an eco-resort. Located close to the continental shelf, the island is washed by blue water and visited by a wonderful array of fishes.

More than a dozen dive sites are found around the island, with The Blowhole one of the best on the more exposed eastern side. This side has extensive hard-coral gardens and a wall dropping from 14m to 25m, which is undercut by many caves and ledges. The Blowhole is the biggest of these caves – a large L-shaped tube from the top of the reef to the wall.

In The Blowhole, divers will see angelfish, squirrelfish, sweetlips, coral trout, gropers and occasionally a resting Tawny Nurse Shark or Tasselled Wobbegong. However, the main shark action happens on the wall, as Silvertip Sharks, Whitetip Reef Sharks and Grey Reef Sharks patrol here. Off the wall, divers are also likely to see barracuda, batfish, trevally and maybe a Reef Manta Ray.

The ledges and caves provide shelter for dense schools of glassfish, sweepers and cardinalfish, and feeding off them are packs of Mangrove Jacks and Brassy Trevally. These predatory fish duck in and out of the caves, hoping to corner a few small fish.

Also hunting along this wall are Pacific Trumpetfish. These elongated fish present in two colour morphs, either yellow or brown. They have a very sneaky hunting technique, hiding behind other fish. You often see Pacific Trumpetfish hanging very close to large fish, shadowing them as they swim across the reef. They use this cover

Mangrove Jack (*Lutjanus argentimaculatus*) and Brassy Trevally (*Caranx papuensis*).

Pacific Trumpetfish (*Aulostomus chinensis*).

to get close to small fish and then lunge out and suck up some poor victim. They also ambush prey, staying very still until a small fish gets within range of its snout.

The coral gardens at The Blowhole swarm with reef fishes. Commonly seen are hawkfish, damsels, parrotfish, surgeonfish, pufferfish, wrasses, angelfish and goatfish. Huge numbers of Blue Tang are seen here, but they disappear into coral hiding spots when a diver gets too close. A good variety of butterflyfish are also on show, including pairs of Bluespot Butterflyfish. These pretty fish can be observed feeding on coral polyps as they make their way slowly across the reef. However, they and other butterflyfish have also been observed cleaning other fish, picking off parasites.

Bluespot Butterflyfish (*Chaetodon plebeius*).

24 LIGHTHOUSE BOMMIES, LADY ELLIOT ISLAND

The western side of Lady Elliot Island is more sheltered from ocean swells, and features coral gardens in the shallows and a sandy plain dotted with bommies. All of these bommies make for great diving. However, Lighthouse Bommies is the most popular site, as it is the best place to see Lady Elliot Island's most famous residents – Reef Manta Rays.

There are numerous spots in Australia where you can see Reef Manta Rays, with researchers discovering that Lady Elliot Island has the biggest population. These huge rays can grow to 5.5m in width and have a very wide mouth to feed on their favourite meal of plankton. Reef Manta Rays visit Lighthouse Bommies to get cleaned, and with hundreds of these giant rays visiting the island, there can sometimes be a queue for this service. Mantas are intelligent and curious animals, and will often come very close to inspect divers. Lighthouse Bommies is an ideal spot to sit on the bottom and watch these majestic creatures.

The numerous coral heads at Lighthouse Bommies sit in 8m to 15m of water and

Bicolor Angelfish (*Centropyge bicolor*).

Reef Manta Ray (*Mobula alfredi*).

are surrounded by a sandy plain. This sand is home to a colony of Spotted Garden Eels, and is a good location to see gobies, goatfish, flounders and stingrays. Leopard Shark and Whitespotted Wedgefish also rest here and use the cleaning services of the Common Cleaner Wrasse.

These bommies also attract Spotted Eagle Ray, Whitetip Reef Shark, batfish, trevally, barracuda and mackerel. Numerous ledges and crevices cut the bommies and provide shelter for rockcods, morays and Tasselled Wobbegong.

A good variety of reef fishes call this site home, including butterflyfish, sweetlips, surgeonfish, fusiliers, basslets, parrotfish, hawkfish, pufferfish and rabbitfish. This is a good spot to see Bicolor Angelfish. This pretty fish is a type of pygmy angelfish, with most individuals less than 10cm long. They differ from the larger angelfish, which are always seen in male/female pairs, in that the male has a harem of females, which can number up to seven. If the male dies, the most dominant female will change sex to take his place. Bicolor Angelfish are always entertaining to watch, and also tricky to photograph as they rarely stay still and don't like to be cornered.

While the big fish get most of the attention at Lighthouse Bommies, taking a

Leaf Scorpionfish (*Taenianotus triacanthus*).

close look between the corals can be very rewarding. I have seen numerous blennies, gobies, pipefish and even dragonets. And this is also a good spot to see Leaf Scorpionfish. These gorgeous little fish are well camouflaged, so not easy to spot, and are often found in pairs. Leaf Scorpionfish are ambush predators that wait very patiently for prey to come within range so it can be snatched. They often get algae growing on their skin, and to deal with this they moult every few weeks. When they moult, they can also change colour, so you can see them in white, yellow, pink, cream or brown.

One million years ago a volcano erupted at Bundaberg, creating Queensland's best shore-diving location. The eruption blasted basalt rocks throughout the area, creating a rocky shoreline that is now covered in corals and fishes.

There are several dive sites off Bundaberg which offer fabulous snorkelling and diving, with my favourite being Barolin Rocks. The entry and exit at this site is via a rock pool, but take care as the rocks can be slippery. The rocky reef at Barolin Rocks is only 2m to 9m deep, and covered in soft corals, hard corals and some lovely gorgonians.

Residing in these coral gardens are angelfish, butterflyfish, wrasses, pufferfish, boxfish, gobies, morays, sweetlips, rockcods, damsels and goatfish. Pelagic fish occasional visit the site, including trevally, barracuda and batfish. This is also a good spot to see a few sharks and rays, with Australian Bluespotted Maskrays and Eastern Shovelnose Rays resting under the sand and Greater Bamboo Sharks hiding between the rocks.

The most common shark here is Ornate Wobbegong. These small sharks only grow to 1.1m long, and until recently they and the much larger Banded Wobbegong were considered to be the same species, although strangely with very different

Ornate Wobbegong (*Orectolobus ornatus*).

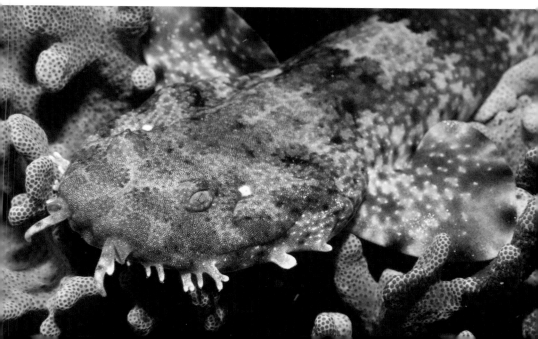

Left: Longspine Porcupinefish
(*Tragulichthys jaculiferus*).

Below: Ringscale Threefin
(*Enneapterygius atrogulare*).

patterns. This was finally sorted out by researchers, even though many divers for years suspected that they were two different species. The Ornate Wobbegong spends much of the day, and most of the night, simply resting on the bottom, tucked up between corals. Like all wobbegongs they are ambush predators, and wait for prey (anything big enough to fit in their mouth) to swim by. Juvenile Ornate Wobbegongs are often seen at Barolin Rocks. However, they tend to be more cryptic, to avoid being eaten by larger wobbies!

The rocky bottom at Barolin Rocks forms many ledges and gullies, where porcupinefish like to hide. Porcupinefish are closely related to pufferfish, although with larger spines and with their teeth fused together to form a beak-like jaw. Around a dozen species are found in Australian waters, with the Shortspine Porcupinefish the most common species seen at Barolin Rocks. However, I have also seen a rarer Longspine Porcupinefish at this site. Porcupinefish are slow swimmers, and to avoid predators they have poisonous flesh and can inflate themselves into a spiky ball!

One of the best features of Barolin Rocks is its small fishes. This is a spot where you take your time and closely inspect the corals, rocks and ledges looking for gobies, blennies and threefins. A good population of Ringscale Threefin is found at this site. These little fish are often mistaken for gobies, except they have a pointed snout and three dorsal fins. The Ringscale Threefin grows to 6cm in length, and while the females are a dull green-brown colour, the males are brightly coloured in red and black.

26 COCHRANE ARTIFICIAL REEF, BUNDABERG

Offshore from Bundaberg is a collection of rocky reefs that offers exceptional diving. However, closer to shore is an artificial reef that swarms with fishes – the Cochrane Artificial Reef.

It was started in 1992 with the sinking of several old gravel barges, a trawler, lightships, pontoons and three planes. These now rest on the sandy bottom in depths from 14m to 18m. A block trail between each scuttled structure allows for easy navigation. The old ships and planes are fun to explore and provide a home for a great variety of fishes.

Leopard Whipray (*Himantura leoparda*).

Chinamanfish (*Symphorus nematophorus*).

Commonly seen fishes include Spotted Eagle Ray, batfish, trevally, barracuda, mackerel, sweetlips, wobbegongs and Whitetip Reef Shark. The sandy plain between each structure is a good place to encounter a variety of stingrays. I have seen Australian Bluespotted Maskray, Blotched Fantail Stingray and Pink Whipray. However, a highlight on one dive was seeing what I suspect was a large Leopard Whipray. According to researchers this species is not found off the east coast of Australia. However, I have photographed a few off southern Queensland with the distinctive leopard-like pattern. I am currently waiting on researchers to obtain DNA samples from this east-coast species, to confirm it is in fact a Leopard Whipray.

Many reef fishes populate the structures at Cochrane Artificial Reef, including a good assortment of butterflyfish, angelfish, goatfish, wrasses, rockcods, damsels, morays, scorpionfish, surgeonfish, tuskfish, pufferfish and parrotfish. Numerous coral snappers are seen swarming around the wrecks, including schools of Bigeye and Blackspot Coral Snapper. You can even see the two prettiest members of this family here, the Red Emperor Snapper and Chinamanfish. I'm not sure how the Chinamanfish got its strange name, as it is a very attractive fish with its blue stripes and long filaments trailing from its dorsal fin.

Gropers are particularly abundant, with plenty of food and hiding spots. Dozens

Queensland Groper (*Epinephelus lanceolatus*).

of Goldspotted Gropers are seen on every dive, and this site is also home to the largest member of this family, the enormous Queensland Groper. Officially reported to reach lengths of 2.7m, I have seen a few that were easily more than 3m long! These huge fish feed on almost anything they can catch and swallow – everything from crabs to fish to sharks and even turtles!

Queensland Gropers are usually shy and wary of divers, so you can rarely get close to one unless you suddenly surprise it inside a wreck. Two or three can generally be seen on Cochrane Artificial Reef as you swim from wreck to wreck. This species appears to spawn during winter, with groups seen together at this time of year.

27 WOLF ROCK, RAINBOW BEACH

Wolf Rock is one of the most action-packed dive sites in Australia. Located 1km off Double Island Point, near the town of Rainbow Beach, this rocky pinnacle is almost constantly washed by currents and attracts fish like a magnet.

Rising from 33m, the five peaks of Wolf Rock align from east to west, with the two western pinnacles breaking the surface. Around the pinnacle are gutters, crevices and ledges to explore that are decorated by sponges, soft corals, hard corals and black coral trees.

Wolf Rock is most famous for its resident population of Grey Nurse Sharks, which occupy the site year-round. The east-coast Grey Nurse Shark population migrates annually, with the sharks spending summer in New South Wales and heading north to Queensland for the winter. It was thought very strange that large numbers of these sharks were seen here during summer until it was recently discovered that they were all pregnant females. This makes Wolf Rock the only known Grey Nurse Shark maternity ward! While numbers vary throughout the year, at peak times up to 100 of these magnificent sharks can be observed. Watching Grey Nurse Sharks is an easy exercise as they are very placid and curious. Divers are asked not to block their swim-path or harass these endangered sharks.

Grey Nurse Shark (*Carcharias taurus*).

Goldspotted Groper (*Epinephelus coioides*).

These are not the only sharks seen at Wolf Rock, as divers can also see Spotted Wobbegong, Blacktip Reef Shark and Leopard Shark during summer. Rays are also seen in large numbers, with Pink Whipray and Blotched Fantail Stingray common. Reef Manta Rays also visit, with autumn the best time for an encounter. Even the very rare Bowmouth Wedgefish and Ornate Eagle Ray can sometimes make an appearance.

My favourite rays here are the Spotted Eagle Rays, which cruise around the peaks, often in large fevers. This species is found in both tropical and subtropical waters around Australia and grows to 3m in width. They are mostly observed cruising in midwater, but feed on the bottom on crustaceans and other invertebrates.

Besides all the sharks and rays, Wolf Rock is constantly surrounded by schools of pelagic fish, including trevally, barracuda, mackerel, bonito, batfish, Yellowtail Kingfish and Cobia. Schools of fusiliers, surgeonfish and coral snappers also add to the large volume of fishes.

A great assortment of reef fish includes various angelfish, butterflyfish, rabbitfish, damsels, morays, scorpionfish, rockcods, wrasses, parrotfish, tuskfish and goatfish. Wolf Rock is also home to some very large Queensland Gropers, although divers are more likely to see Goldspotted Groper. These large fish grow to 1.2m in length and are quite tolerant of divers, especially when they are visiting a cleaning station. They are also known as Estuary Gropers, as they like to hang out in estuaries, especially when they are young. As the young Goldspotted Gropers grow they can either mature as males, or as females that later turn into males as they get bigger. This makes them diandric protogynous hermaphrodites. Goldspotted Gropers are known to form into large schools to spawn, although this hasn't been observed in Australia.

A few unique fish can be seen at Wolf Rock every now and then, including frogfish, ghostpipefish, snake eels and stonefish.

Spotted Eagle Ray (*Aetobatus ocellatus*).

28 THE PINNACLE, JEW SHOAL, NOOSA

The Sunshine Coast has many wonderful dive sites. Mooloolaba, with several dive shops, is the most popular destination with divers. While off Noosa is a brilliant rocky reef covered in coral called Jew Shoal. This reef has several dive sites, with the main feature being a rocky ridge called The Pinnacle, which rises from 17m to 5m.

Exploring this ridge, divers will find caves, crevices, ledges and gutters. These are in turn encrusted with soft corals, black corals, gorgonians and hard corals. Covering this reef are often vast schools of bullseyes and yellowtail, and feasting on them are trevally, barracuda and mackerel.

Ornate and Spotted Wobbegongs are commonly seen resting on the bottom, and hiding under ledges can be Tawny Nurse Shark and Greater Bamboo Shark. Stingrays and Spotted Eagle Ray also visit Jew Shoal.

Finespot Wrasse (*Cirrhilabrus punctatus*).

Harlequin Tuskfish (*Choerodon fasciatus*).

A great variety of reef fishes are seen on all parts of this reef. Expect to see a wide assortment of butterflyfish, damsels, angelfish, lizardfish, porcupinefish, grubfish, surgeonfish, morays, leatherjackets, pufferfish, scorpionfish, lionfish and goatfish. It is also a good spot to find Harlequin Tuskfish; these colourful fish are best seen in the many caves looking for a meal, which can include crustaceans, molluscs, worms or echinoderms. Dentally challenged, Harlequin Tuskfish have teeth that protrude out of their mouth, like tusks, which are designed to help them grip prey. They are mostly seen alone on the reef, which is strange as they are thought to form

Blackchest Shrimp Goby (*Amblyeleotris guttata*).

monogamous pairs. If you are very lucky you might even see a juvenile Harlequin Tuskfish, which can be identified by the eye-spots on their fins.

Like all reefs off southern Queensland, a huge variety of wrasses can be seen on every dive. Common species include Green Moon, Gunther's, Birdnose, Blackbarred, Leopard and Redblotched Wrasse. One of my favourites is the Finespot Wrasse – a lovely fish with a pattern of fine blue spots, which can be easily overlooked as it only grows to 13cm in length. Often seen in small groups comprising a male and his harem of females, Finespot Wrasse also mix with other small fishes as they move across the reef, enjoying safety in numbers.

Jew Shoal is also a good spot to see blennies, sand gobies, glider gobies and shrimp gobies. On the shrimp goby front you have a chance of observing Broad-banded, Burgundy and Blackchest Shrimp Gobies and their housemate shrimps. In one of the oddest pairings underwater, shrimp gobies share a home with snapping shrimps. This strange commensal relationship is always interesting to observe, with the shrimp goby standing guard while the snapping shrimps maintain the home. If a predator gets too close, the goby waves its tail or starts to back up, a warning for the shrimp to retreat. They both benefit from this 'odd couple' relationship.

29 MUDJIMBA ISLAND, MOOLOOLABA

Located only one kilometre offshore, Mudjimba Island is a popular spot for divers and snorkellers as it is ringed by a rocky reef covered in coral. Unfortunately, it is also close to the mouth of the Maroochy River, so it doesn't always have the best visibility. However, it is easy to put up with some murky water to see the wonderful fishes at this site.

The coral gardens at Mudjimba are very beautiful and should really be protected as a marine reserve with moorings as boat anchors regularly damage the corals. These healthy coral gardens play host to a wonderful variety of fish. In depths from 3m to 8m, divers will see an assortment of butterflyfish, angelfish, wrasses, tangs, damsels, surgeonfish, rabbitfish, parrotfish, morwongs, sweetlips and goatfish. Schools of stripeys, bullseyes and Diamondfish often cover the reef in places. Spotted and Ornate Wobbegongs are also common.

On the western side of the island the reef drops to 12m, and this boulder wall is

Australian Butterfly Ray (*Gymnura australis*).

a good spot to see squirrelfish, hawkfish, lionfish, rockcods, blennies, scorpionfish and morays. A number of moray species reside in the many ledges, including the occasional Whitemouth Moray – an attractive moray with a white polka-dot pattern and, as the name suggests, a white mouth.

Another fish found hiding in the nooks and crannies of this boulder wall is the Northern Blue Devil. Blue devils are only found in Australian waters, with the family containing five members. Two species are well known to temperate divers, while the Northern Blue Devil is a lesser-known subtropical cousin. Only found off southern Queensland, the Northern Blue Devil is rarely seen, except at Mudjimba. With a little searching you can easily find several sitting under ledges propped up on their long-fins.

Most divers stick to the wall and reef, but if you venture onto the sand and rubble you will find some interesting fishes. This is where flatheads, goatfish, grubfish, lizardfish, glider gobies, flounders, shrimp gobies and even grinners can be found. However, it is the rays that most impress. Common Stingaree and Australian

Whitemouth Moray (*Gymnothorax meleagris*).

Northern Blue Devil (*Paraplesiops poweri*).

Bluespotted Maskray are the most abundant, with dozens found resting on the sand. I have also found this a great spot to see Eastern Shovelnose Ray.

The rarest ray I have seen at Mudjimba is the Australian Butterfly Ray, which grows to 1m in width and looks like a giant taco with a very short banded tail. This species is sandy in colour and also incredibly flat, making it very hard to spot when buried in the sand. Fortunately, the one I encountered at Mudjimba was resting above the sand and allowed me to observe and photograph it for several minutes. In 40 years of diving and fishwatching, I have only seen two of these strange rays.

The guided-missile destroyer HMAS *Brisbane* had a long and illustrious career. For the ship's retirement it could have easily been sold for scrap metal. Fortunately, the Australian government decided to give the vessel a second career, as an artificial reef. The ship was scuttled off Mooloolaba in 2005 and is today one of the best fishwatching spots in Australia.

Resting on a sandy plain in 27m of water, the 133m-long ship is the only structure for miles around, so quickly developed into an important fish habitat. The sand around the ship attracts Pink Whipray, Blotched Fantail Stingray, Whitespotted Wedgefish, goatfish, grubfish and flatheads. A school of Mulloway mill around the stern, and are often joined by barracuda, trevally and sweetlips. The sand is also the best place to see the resident Queensland Gropers. They sleep in the ship at night, and when divers visit they like to patrol the sand.

The ship itself is decorated by corals and sponges, and it supports a vast array of fishes. Commonly observed are wrasses, angelfish, butterflyfish, rockcods, leatherjackets, tuskfish, pufferfish, parrotfish, hawkfish, scorpionfish, lionfish,

Lilac-tip Basslet (*Pseudanthias rubrizonatus*).

Capricorn Cardinalfish (*Ostorhinchus capricornis*) with a mouthful of eggs.

damsels and goatfish. I often sit on the bow and simply watch the endless parade of reef fish moving in and out of the corals and across the deck.

One of the most colourful reef fish found on the ship is the Lilac-tip Basslet. The male of this species is a rainbow of colours with a striking red bar along its side, while the female is reddish pink. They mainly eat zooplankton and can be observed darting back and forth as they search for these little food particles.

Above all these reef fishes is a constant parade of pelagic fish – Yellowtail Kingfish, Longfin Batfish, Australasian Snapper, mackerel and a huge variety of trevally. And joining in this mass of fish are Spotted Eagle Rays.

Inside the ship is where millions of baitfish shelter, including sweepers, sprats, glassfish and cardinalfish. These fish are easily overlooked, except the cardinalfish, which are definitely worth your time as they are mouth brooders. The main species seen here is the Capricorn Cardinalfish, and if you look for ones with a swollen jaw, they may be holding eggs. If you wait patiently, they regularly open and close their mouth to oxygenate the eggs, and often they spit them out entirely to give them a proper flush.

Gobies and blennies are seen on HMAS *Brisbane*, and the ship also attracts frogfish. Over the years I have seen Striate, Giant and Painted Frogfish. As these strange fish don't swim much, preferring to walk with their hand-like fins, it is thought that they arrive on the ship as larvae. However, they are extremely well camouflaged, so can be seen for a few weeks in one spot and then simply disappear. The longest-staying residents were a pair of Painted Frogfish that lingered for several months. This species grows to 30cm in length and comes in a range of colours that offer camouflage against the bottom substrate.

Painted Frogfish (*Antennarius pictus*).

31 FLINDERS REEF, BRISBANE

Brisbane has some of the best subtropical diving in the world, with dozens of rocky reefs and shipwrecks covered in coral and fishes. I may be a little biased when it comes to Brisbane, as this is where I live and do most of my diving. However, anyone who has dived this area will know it has fabulous diving off Moreton Island and North Stradbroke Island. The most popular spot off Moreton Island is Flinders Reef.

This rocky reef has so much coral coverage that it looks like a true coral reef. Protected as a marine sanctuary, with no anchoring allowed, moorings are located around the reef to preserve the delicate coral. While you can dive and snorkel right around Flinders Reef, the best spot for fishwatching is in the shallow coral gardens on the western side. Sheltered from swells, gardens of staghorn coral flourish here, and there are also many ledges and crevices to explore.

A wealth of reef fish can be seen at Flinders Reef, including a good diversity of goatfish, coral snappers, rockcods, wrasses, sweetlips, morwongs, morays, damsels,

Threeband Butterflyfish (*Chaetodon tricinctus*).

Lemonpeel Pearlscale Hybrid Angelfish (*Centropyge flavissima × vrolikii*).

anemonefish, gobies, blennies, lionfish, scorpionfish, leatherjackets, surgeonfish, tangs, pufferfish, hawkfish, grubfish and porcupinefish. Schools of trevally, barracuda and batfish swim through regularly, and divers will also see stingrays, wobbegongs and even Whitetip Reef Shark in summer, and the occasional Grey Nurse Shark during winter. Flinders Reef is also a great spot to see Australia's most common electric ray, the Coffin Ray.

Beautiful butterflyfish are seen in large numbers. Most of these are common tropical species, although a rare endemic species to look for is the Threeband Butterflyfish. This gorgeous little fish is only found across a limited area of northern New South Wales and southern Queensland. The ones I have seen were quite shy, sheltering under ledges, so easily missed. They may also be territorial, as I saw one Threeband Butterflyfish hanging around the same ledge at Flinders Reef for more than six months.

A great variety of angelfish also call the reef home, including Coral Beauty, Bicolor, Keyhole and Blue Angelfish. Two of the prettiest pygmy angelfish seen here

Harlequin Filefish (*Oxymonacanthus longirostris*).

are the Pearlscale and Lemonpeel. These two species are around the same size, up to 12cm long, and are often seen together darting in and out of ledges. They seem to like each other's company so much they interbreed, producing offspring known as the Lemonpeel Pearlscale Hybrid Angelfish. These offspring have a colour pattern that is a blend of both parents and they are worth looking out for at Flinders Reef.

Some special fishes turn up at Flinders Reef on occasion, such as Giant Frogfish, Tawny Nurse Shark, Sicklefin Lemon Shark and even a few dragonets. However, a very special fish that can be seen on almost every dive is the Harlequin Filefish. The prettiest member of the leatherjacket family, these colourful fish are nearly always seen in pairs swimming among the staghorn corals. They feed on acropora coral polyps, and strangely take on the smell of the coral. This cloaks the fish's natural smell to deter predators, and they are the only fish species known to do this. Fortunately, we can't smell them underwater, so simply take joy in watching these lovely fish weave between the corals.

32 HENDERSON ROCK, BRISBANE

The outer side of Moreton Island has a few hidden rocky reefs that can only be dived when conditions are calm, as they are exposed to ocean swells and often washed by strong currents. However, when conditions are calm, especially during winter, these reefs offer exceptional diving and fish life.

I could easily list five of these dive sites as hot-spots for fishwatching, but I will stick with one – the always-brilliant Henderson Rock. The main feature at this site is a large gutter that ends in a cave. However, there are also ledges, ridges and overhangs to explore in depths from 12m to 30m.

In winter this is a great spot to observe Grey Nurse Sharks. Both males and heavily pregnant females can be encountered, with most doing slow circuits of the gutter. Anywhere from two to twenty sharks can be seen. Henderson Rock is also home to dozens of Banded, Spotted and Ornate Wobbegongs. Squadrons of Spotted Eagle Rays like to cruise around the rock, especially when a current is running. The currents also attract schools of barracuda, trevally, batfish and surgeonfish.

While a good mixture of reef fishes can be found, the main reason I love this spot for fishwatching is for the rare and unusual fish that turn up here from time

Sculptured Toadfish (*Halophryne queenslandiae*).

Conspicuous Angelfish (*Chaetodontoplus conspicillatus*).

to time. On one dive I made a great discovery of a Sculptured Toadfish sheltering under a ledge. While everyone else was busy watching the sharks, I got down low to study this weird little fish as it was only the second time I had seen this rare species.

In Australia these fishes are also confusingly called frogfish, although with a face like a toad and having the ability to croak, toadfish is a far more appropriate name. Nine species of these cryptic fish are found around Australia, with the Sculptured Toadfish found off Queensland and northern New South Wales. The male is a fabulous father, as he guards the eggs the female deposits in his lair until they hatch, and even after they hatch has been observed guarding the tiny offspring. I have seen many toadfish over the years, although sadly I have never seen these wonderful dads in action.

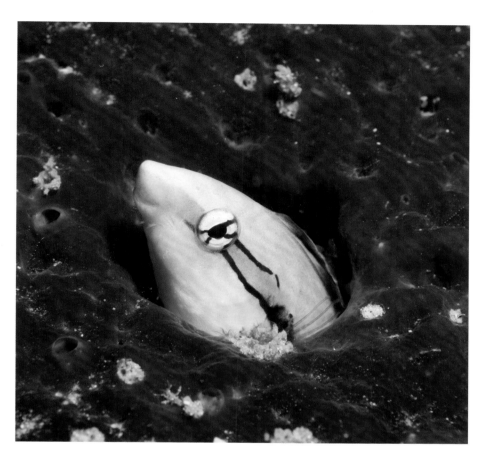

False Cleaner Blenny (*Aspidontus taeniatus*).

Another rare fish I have observed at Henderson Rock is the Conspicuous Angelfish. This elegant species is found off southern Queensland and northern New South Wales, although it is rarely seen, preferring deeper reefs. It grows to 25cm in length and feeds on tunicates and sponges. They are generally seen in pairs, but the one I encountered at Henderson Rock was all by itself.

There are several fish cleaning stations at Henderson Rock where you can watch Common Cleaner Wrasse performing their chores. However, you can also see a fish that mimics these cleaners, the False Cleaner Blenny. These cheeky fish have adopted a similar colour pattern to the Common Cleaner Wrasse, so they can pretend to be one of the cleaner crew. However, when they get close to the unsuspecting client, they nip a mouthful of flesh and then retreat to their lair!

33 CURTIN ARTIFICAL REEF, BRISBANE

Inside Moreton Bay are several interesting dive sites, including the world's first artificial reef created by divers for divers. Curtin Artificial Reef was started by the Underwater Research Group of Queensland in 1968, when they scuttled a barge off Cowan Point, Moreton Island. Over the years they added more than 30 vessels, concrete pipes, tyres and other objects. The reef is in depths from 12m to 30m and swarms with fish life.

The wrecks are enjoyable to explore and best dived on the high tide as the site is tidal. As soon as you descend onto any of the wrecks you will be greeted by Queensland Gropers. Dozens of these giant fish live on the wrecks, and they have become very friendly over the years. On some dives you will find yourself being followed by six or more of these massive fish.

Purple Tuskfish (*Choerodon cephalotes*).

False Scorpionfish (*Centrogenys vaigiensis*).

The gropers are here in large numbers as the wrecks provide a home and plenty of food. Schools of pelagic fish circle the wrecks, including a variety of trevally, batfish, barracuda and surgeonfish. Each of these wrecks is home to masses of reef fish, including a range of wrasses, angelfish, butterflyfish, pufferfish, damsels, hawkfish, rockcods, lionfish, morays, sweetlips, parrotfish, rabbitfish, emperors and soapfish.

An endemic fish always seen here is the Purple Tuskfish. Like other tuskfish, this species doesn't have the most attractive-looking teeth. However, they serve a purpose, allowing the fish to feed on crabs, sea urchins and molluscs. Purple Tuskfish are often observed lifting rubble with these teeth while searching for a meal. They grow to 35cm in length and have a lovely blue banded pattern on the head, with not a patch of purple to be seen, so the origin of that common name is unclear. Purple Tuskfish are generally observed alone, only pairing up when breeding.

The wrecks of Curtin Artificial Reef are usually a good spot to see elasmobranchs. Spotted Wobbegongs rest on the wrecks, while Spotted Eagle Rays patrol above. The sand between the wrecks is the place to see Blotched Fantail Stingray, Pink Whipray and Broad Cowtail Stingray.

A few unusual fish can be seen at this site, including the occasional frogfish,

Blackspot Waspfish (*Liocranium praepositum*).

stonefish and sole. One of the most interesting and unusual species here is the False Scorpionfish, which sits camouflaged on the bottom looking like a scorpionfish, but is in fact a member of the groper family. They mimic scorpionfish to avoid larger predators, and use their camouflage to ambush small fish and crustaceans. The False Scorpionfish prefers estuary habitats, and Curtin Artificial Reef fits this bill, as dozens can be seen sitting on the wrecks.

Another unusual fish seen here is the Blackspot Waspfish. Not a lot is known about this fish, other than it is endemic to southern Queensland and rarely seen. However, they are found quite regularly at this site, sitting on the bottom waiting to ambush prey. Waspfish are members of the scorpionfish family, with venomous spines. Look for Blackspot Waspfish under the wrecks and among the shell debris.

34 TURTLE CAVES, FLAT ROCK, BRISBANE

Flat Rock is located off North Stradbroke Island and is where divers go to see big fish off Brisbane. There are three main dive sites: the Shark Gutters at the southern end, the Aquarium on the west and Turtle Caves at the northern end. Years ago, I would have nominated the Shark Gutters as the best site for fishwatching, because of the gathering of Grey Nurse Sharks here each winter. However, my favourite now is Turtle Caves.

The sloping rocky reef at Turtle Caves drops from 6m to 30m, and is cut with gutters, overhangs and many ledges. The corals here are very colourful, a mix of hard corals, soft corals, black corals and gorgonians. And swarming around these corals are masses of fish.

The big fish are the most obvious. Grey Nurse Sharks patrol here during

Blue Tang (*Paracanthurus hepatus*).

Eastern Morwong (*Goniistius vestitus*).

winter, while summer sees Whitetip Reef Sharks and Leopard Sharks making an appearance. Lots of wobbegongs rest all over the reef, and divers also have a chance of seeing Bull Shark and Tawny Nurse Shark. Spotted Eagle Rays are very common, especially when a current is present. They can also be joined by schools of Australian Cownose Rays and even the occasional Giant Devilray. This is also a spot where anything can turn up, including Bowmouth Wedgefish, Great Hammerhead and even a Whale Shark.

Schools of trevally, batfish, barracuda and surgeonfish mingle in the current, and divers are also likely to see mackerel, bonito and Yellowtail Kingfish. The big fish action can be mesmerising, but it is the smaller fish that I most enjoy at Turtle Caves.

Among the boulders expect to see damsels, sweetlips, angelfish, hawkfish, butterflyfish, boxfish, pufferfish, morays, goatfish, squirrelfish, cardinalfish, wrasses, rockcods and basslets. One of my favourites here are the Blue Tangs. Dozens of these attractive fish live on the reef and can be seen feeding on plankton. If disturbed they quickly disperse to their hiding spots, with the larger ones retiring to crevices and

Halfmoon Triggerfish (*Rhinecanthus lunula*).

the small ones wedging between the branches of hard coral. They are reported to live in groups of up to 14, a mix of males and females, and when they spawn, they change to a pale blue colour and swim off the bottom to release their eggs and sperm.

A very common species seen at Turtle Caves is the Eastern Morwong. More than a dozen species of morwong are found in Australian waters, and all have thick lips, long pectoral fins and pretty colour patterns. Morwongs are mostly found in temperate waters, although a few also reside in the subtropics. The Eastern Morwong is the most common member of the family seen off southern Queensland, and like its cousins it spends most of the day lazing on the bottom, often in large groups.

Unusual reef fish turn up at Turtle Caves on occasions, such as frogfish, Leaf Scorpionfish, pipefish, dragonets and even a Lacy Scorpionfish. However, I got a wonderful surprise when I recently spotted a Halfmoon Triggerfish. Little is known about this attractive fish, as sightings are very rare.

35 SHAG ROCK, BRISBANE

S hag Rock is a little on the nose. A popular spot for roosting seabirds, the rock smells of bird poo if you get too close. It is also on the nose with divers, as it is always the last choice of dive site off North Stradbroke Island. It doesn't have the best corals, but for any fishwatcher this is a great spot to see a wonderful variety of fabulous fishes. The rocky reef around Shag Rock varies in depth from 3m to 18m. The site has walls, gutters, ledges and stacks of boulders.

All sides of Shag Rock offer great diving, with the northern side my favourite. I aways start my dives out on the sand, as this is where you see rays. Common Stingaree, Australian Bluespotted Maskray and Blotched Fantail Stingray are the most common species seen, with this also a good place to see Coffin Ray. Also look for goatfish, flounders, flatheads and gobies. Recently I got a big surprise when I spotted a small colony of Spotted Garden Eels, which are well south of their normal range.

While pelagic fishes visit this rocky reef, it is the reef fishes that are the main attraction. Schools of bullseyes, fusiliers and scad often cover the reef, and expect

Barred Moray (*Echidna polyzona*).

Honeycomb Toby (*Canthigaster janthinoptera*).

to see wobbegongs and Greater Bamboo Shark hiding in ledges. Typical reef fishes include varieties of wrasses, angelfish, anemonefish, damsels, lionfish, morwongs, sweetlips, boxfish, surgeonfish and a good population of morays. The most unusual moray seen here is the Barred Moray. Unlike most morays, this species has blunt stumpy teeth, as they prefer to feed on crustaceans and use these teeth to crush their shells.

One of the main highlights of Shag Rock are the porcupinefish and pufferfish, with hundreds seen on a dive. This is a wonderful spot to also see tobies, with Blackspot, Pacific Crown, Blacksaddle and the gorgeous Honeycomb Tobies common. Tobies are the smallest members of the pufferfish family, with most only growing to 10cm in length. They feed on everything from algae to small invertebrates, and some are shy and hidden away, while others boldly swim around the reef. The Honeycomb Toby is on the shy side, so look under ledges for this very attractive fish.

Shag Rock is also a great spot to see weird and wonderful fishes. Horrid Stonefish, False Stonefish, Leaf Scorpionfish, Painted Frogfish, dragonets, ghostpipefish and even Cockatoo Waspfish have been observed here. I was lucky enough to find an unusual clingfish at Shag Rock. Clingfish are tiny scaleless fish that cling to objects

Undescribed clingfish (*Lepadichthys* species).

using a sucking disk formed by modified pelvic fins. Australia is home to 28 species of these strange little fish, and most are rarely seen. I found this little clingfish swimming among the spines of a sea urchin, and thought it was a Doublestriped Clingfish. However, a recent review of the family found that the Doublestriped Clingfish is limited to the Indian Ocean, and the species I found is most likely undescribed.

36 MANTA BOMMIE, BRISBANE

This is one of my favourite dive sites in Australia, and it certainly is an incredible spot for sharks and rays. In my opinion it has been misnamed. Sure, this is a great spot to see Reef Manta Rays, but the real stars are the Leopard Sharks, so some divers have nicknamed it Leopard Shark Bommie.

Manta Bommie is located at The Group, a collection of rocks off North Stradbroke Island. The rocky reef at this site varies from 3m to 12m, with several bommies serving as cleaning stations. The edge of the reef then drops to a sandy plain, 15m deep. Manta Bommie is often washed by strong currents and plagued by poor visibility. However, when conditions are good it is one of the best dive sites in Australia.

The site comes alive each November when the Reef Manta Rays and other visitors arrive for the summer, and quietens down again by May when they depart. The mantas visit the cleaning stations to get cleaned, and anywhere from two to a

Leopard Shark (*Stegostoma tigrinum*).

Whitespotted Wedgefish (*Rhynchobatus australiae*).

dozen can be seen at peak times. They are often joined by Spotted Eagle Rays, which take great delight soaring around the reef.

While the mantas are wonderful, it is the Leopard Sharks that are the true stars, with researchers discovering that more than 400 individuals use this site for resting, feeding and possibly breeding. These attractive sharks spend their days resting on the sand, and anywhere from 10 to 50 can be seen, making Manta Bommie the most important habitat for these sharks anywhere in the world.

Joining the Leopard Sharks on the sand are numerous stingrays – Pink Whiprays, Blotched Fantail Stingrays, Broad Cowtail Stingrays, Australian Bluespotted Maskrays and Australian Whiprays. Another ray seen in large numbers is the Whitespotted Wedgefish. Growing to 3m in length, these prehistoric-looking rays are an impressive sight, especially when a row of 10 are lined up side-by-side.

Wobbegongs, Greater Bamboo Shark, pelagic fish and a good range of reef fish are also seen at Manta Bommie. However, with its many ledges and caves I also look for more unusual fishes. Over the years I have seen Horrid Stonefish, Leaf Scorpionfish, pipefish and schools of Striped Catfish. However, another uncommon fish I have often seen here is the Pacific Rockcod. This bright orange fish, covered in fine white dots, is normally found in New South Wales, so the ones I have seen here have strayed over the border. They are a very secretive fish, hiding in caves and ledges, emerging at night to feed on crustaceans.

Pacific Rockcod (*Trachypoma macracanthus*).

37 THE SEAWAY, GOLD COAST

Better known for its theme parks, beaches and nightlife, the Gold Coast also has some wonderful dive sites. Off the coast are rocky reefs and shipwrecks, with one of the best spots for fishwatching being the man-made mouth of the Nerang River, better known as The Seaway.

There are several dive sites at The Seaway. A boat is required to dive The Mouth, which is a good spot for rays and Bull Sharks, while you can jump in from the shore to explore The Pipes and see a great variety of reef fish, pelagic fish and even Queensland Gropers. However, the best spot for unusual fishes is further up the river at The Beach. This beach entry gives access to a boulder wall in depths from 2m to 7m, and is best described as a muck dive.

The Seaway is tidal, so best dived on the high tide for good visibility. Diving from the beach you can see a variety of reef fishes, including many juveniles, such

Tasselled Leatherjacket (*Chaetodermis penicilligerus*).

Mossback Velvetfish (*Paraploactis trachyderma*).

as wrasses, butterflyfish, morays, angelfish, bream, flatheads, whiting, surgeonfish, tobies, boxfish, pufferfish, damsels and rockcods. Leatherjackets are extremely abundant, with Fanbelly and Yellowfin Leatherjackets the most common. However, I have also observed a tiny Taylor's Pygmy Leatherjacket and a bizarre Tasselled Leatherjacket. This strange-looking fish is covered in branch-like growths that aid in camouflage. Although a tropical species, it is mostly seen in estuaries, so divers have encountered them at muck sites off Port Stephens and Perth.

A great variety of scorpionfish are found hidden among the rocks. Over the years I have seen Horrid Stonefish, Caledonian Ghoul, Dwarf Lionfish, Common Lionfish, Leaf Scorpionfish, False Stonefish and even False Scorpionfish. Another fish with spines seen in The Seaway is the Mossback Velvetfish. I am not sure how this family of fish got its name, as the skin is more like sandpaper than velvet. Closely related to scorpionfish, velvetfish also have venomous spines and 21 species have been found in Australia. Like other velvetfish, the Mossback Velvetfish is very cryptic, hiding between rocks and seaweed. They often get algae growing on their skin, giving them a mossy appearance. They are not easy to find, so take your time and investigate every rock that has an eye.

Robust Ghostpipefish (*Solenostomus cyanopterus*).

A great range of unusual fish turn up in The Seaway. I have seen three species of frogfish, four species of pipefish and also a few White's Seahorses. In summer ghostpipefish suddenly appear, with both Ornate and Robust Ghostpipefish seen. These well-camouflaged fish like to hide in the seaweed, so a good eye is needed to spot them. The Robust Ghostpipefish I have seen here are the same colour as the seaweed and develop little weedy filaments. If you find one, or a pair which is often the case, watch them closely as they most likely will be feeding on tiny shrimps.

Sand gobies, shrimp gobies and glider gobies are also common in The Seaway. And this is also a good spot to see dragonets, with Grey-spotted and Finger Dragonets found feeding on the sand. Another strange fish seen here is the Estuary Catfish, and divers have also seen Halfband Snake Eels at night – a species that has eluded me so far.

38 *SCOTTISH PRINCE*, GOLD COAST

On the final leg of a long voyage from Glasgow to Brisbane in 1887, the 64m-long iron barque *Scottish Prince* tragically ran around at Main Beach, Gold Coast, just short of its final destination. The ship quickly became a total loss, sinking in 12m, and is today listed as a historic shipwreck. Like other wrecks sitting on sand, the ship has become a haven for fishes.

The ship has collapsed on itself, with only the bow and stern easily identified, although it is still an interesting dive site. The sand around the wreck is always the best place to start, as rays gather here to feed. I have seen Blotched Fantail Stingray, Broad Cowtail Stingray, Australian Bluespotted Maskray and Australian Whipray. This last species has only recently been described by researchers, as it was confused with other similarly patterned whiprays. It can be quite large, reaching a width of 1.8m, and the spectacular disc pattern can vary from reticulations to spots. I have found that swimming east of the wreck is the best place to find Australian Whiprays.

Horned Blenny (*Parablennius intermedius*).

Australian Whipray (*Himantura australis*).

The wreck itself is often covered in schools of Yellowtail Scad, that form a shroud over the site. They are joined by schools of Diamondfish on the bow. These dense schools naturally attract predators, with trevally, mackerel and bonito often launching bombing raids.

Wobbegongs are seen in large numbers all over the wreck, with dozens of Spotted and Ornate Wobbegongs occupying every available hole. Hidden in the wreckage, divers are also likely to see Greater Bamboo Sharks and the occasional Blind Shark.

A great assortment of reef fish reside on the *Scottish Prince*, with numerous species of wrasses, butterflyfish, angelfish, damsels, surgeonfish, pufferfish, rockcods, goatfish, morwongs, morays and grubfish. Temperate species, more common in New South Wales, are also seen, such as Australian Mado, Red Morwong, Old Wife and Eastern Kelpfish. Juvenile fish are regularly spotted on the wreck, including small Yellow Boxfish, Blue Angelfish and some very cute Scribbled Rabbitfish.

This is a site where you need to watch your hands, as lionfish and scorpionfish are common. Horrid Stonefish like to hide on the wreck, either under the sand or wedged between wreckage. These ugly-looking fish feed at night on fish and crustaceans.

Some unusual fish end up on the *Scottish Prince*. There was a resident Leaf Scorpionfish living on the bow for more than a year, and I have also seen a Sculptured Toadfish and an Australian Pineapplefish hiding under wreckage.

One of my favourite small fish on the wreck is the Horned Blenny. These delightful little fish grow to 12cm long and have two fleshy horns above the eyes. They are mostly observed with their head hanging out of a hole, and if you sit still long enough they will emerge and feed on algae.

Horrid Stonefish (*Synanceia horrida*).

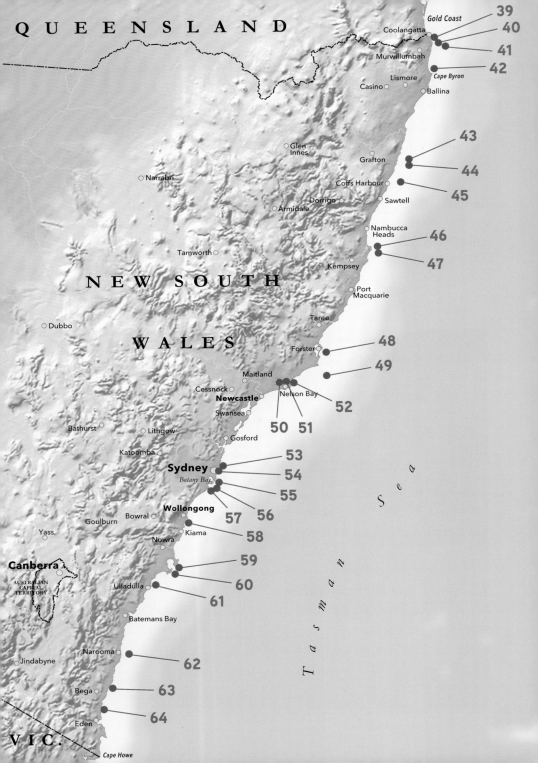

QUEENSLAND

Coolangatta
Gold Coast
39
40
41
Murwillumbah
Cape Byron
42

Lismore
Casino
Ballina

Glen
Innes
43
Grafton
44
Narrabri
Coffs Harbour
45
Dorrigo
Sawtell
Armidale
Nambucca
Heads
46
47
Tamworth
Kempsey

N E W   S O U T H

Port
Macquarie

W A L E S
Taree
Dubbo
Forster
48

49
Maitland
Cessnock
Nelson Bay
52
Newcastle
Swansea
50 **51**
Bathurst
Lithgow
Gosford
Katoomba
53
Sydney
54
Botany Bay
55
Bowral
Wollongong
57 **56**
Goulburn
Kiama
58
Yass
Nowra
59
Canberra
60
AUSTRALIAN
CAPITAL
TERRITORY
Ulladulla
61

Batemans Bay

Narooma
62
Jindabyne
Bega
63
Eden
64

V I C.
Cape Howe

T a s m a n   S e a

NEW SOUTH WALES

The rocky coastline of New South Wales contains some of the best diving and snorkelling sites in the country, and inhabiting these sites is a fabulous variety of tropical and temperate fishes.

The northern part of the state lies in a subtropical zone, with rocky reefs decorated with corals and a multitude of tropical fishes. However, by the time one reaches the mid-north coast, the water temperature cools and you enter the warm temperate zone. This zone, at first, appears similar to the subtropics, but the corals and tropical fish start to thin out and be replaced by temperate fishes and sponge gardens. By the time you reach Sydney and the south coast you are into the temperate zone, and a completely different world of fishes.

The boundaries of these zones are very fuzzy, and with climate change slowly increasing sea temperatures they are creeping further south. Also, the East Australian Current, that washes south from the Great Barrier Reef, brings many tropical fish larvae as far as the south coast. So tropical fish can turn up anywhere in the state, especially during the warmer summer months. Unfortunately, when the water temperature drops in winter, many of these tropical fish die.

With the mixing of subtropical, warm temperate and temperate waters, New South Wales has a fabulous variety of fishes, around 2,050 species in both saltwater and freshwater. Sharks and rays are abundant, and a good variety of pelagic fish are seen at deeper sites or sites washed by currents. The state's rocky reefs, kelp beds and sponge gardens are also populated by a healthy variety of reef fishes, many of which are endemic. New South Wales has several marine reserves, but it could certainly do with many more to protect its unique fish species.

Dive shops and charter boats are located in most of the seaside holiday towns. Many of the popular dive sites in the north of the state are only accessible by boat. However, from Port Stephens south are many brilliant shore-diving sites, where you simply walk in from a beach or scramble across rocks to snorkel or dive. Wherever you explore the underwater world in New South Wales you will have a chance to marvel at a wonderful variety of fishes.

39 TWEED RIVER, TWEED HEADS

Tweed Heads is actually part of the Gold Coast, just stretched over the border into New South Wales. Offshore from Tweed Heads are many wonderful boat-diving sites, however one of the area's most popular dive sites is a shore dive in the Tweed River.

The best spot to dive is near the mouth of the river, at the Jack Evans Boat Harbour. Here steps have been constructed that give easy access to the water for divers and snorkellers. From this spot you can explore a rocky reef in depths to 12m and see an impressive variety of fishes.

Like The Seaway on the Gold Coast, this site is tidal, so best explored on the high tide for minimal water movement and the best visibility. This site doesn't get as many large fish as The Seaway, although it is a great spot to see juvenile fish.

Exploring the rocky reef you will see a good variety of adult and juvenile wrasses,

Oyster Blenny (*Omobranchus anolius*).

Monotone Moray (*Gymnothorax monochrous*).

parrotfish, pufferfish, butterflyfish, coral snappers, rockcods, blennies, goatfish, boxfish, gobies, lionfish, stripeys, leatherjackets, morwong and sweetlips. Some special juvenile fishes to look for include Yellow Boxfish, Painted Sweetlips and pretty Blue Angelfish that have a striking blue-and-white pattern that looks nothing like their parents.

On the sand and rocks numerous small gobies and threefins can be seen. However, I always look for cute Oyster Blennies that hide in the many holes and emerge to quickly dance across the bottom, showing off their flowing fins. These lovely endemic fish grow to 9cm long and are named because they like to hide in empty oyster shells.

The Tweed River is also home to an exceptional variety of morays in the many nooks and crannies. Commonly seen are Highfin, Snowflake and Stout Morays with their heads hanging out of holes. However, I have also seen a rare Monotone Moray in the Tweed River. This is a wide-ranging tropical species, although rarely seen. It is also called the Drab or Brown Moray, due to its plain colouration. I am sure several other moray species also call this site home.

Marbled Fortescue (*Centropogon marmoratus*).

The Tweed River is also a good spot to see large Dusky Flathead, bream, flounders, trevally and a number of scorpionfish. The most common member of the scorpionfish family seen is Marbled Fortescue, which is small and well camouflaged, but still capable of delivering a nasty sting. This species is endemic to this region, between Gladstone and Sydney, and is generally only found in bays and estuaries.

Many weird and wonderful fishes turn up in the Tweed River, including dragonets, pipefish, seahorses, ghostpipefish and frogfish. Both Painted and Striate Frogfish have been seen in the river and when in residence they are very popular with underwater photographers.

40 NORTHERN LEDGES, COOK ISLAND, TWEED HEADS

Cook Island is a dive site that never disappoints. Located off Fingal Head, and south of the Tweed River mouth, it sometimes suffers from poor visibility when dirty water flushes from the river. Surrounded by rocky reefs that are covered in corals, Cook Island is a haven for fish life and protected as a marine sanctuary.

While you can dive right around the island, my favourite spot to fishwatch is the Northern Ledges. Located on the northern side of the island, this site has a boulder wall and a sandy plain dotted with rocky outcrops in depths to 20m. I generally start my dives exploring these rocky outcrops, as some very interesting fishes can be found here.

Between these boulders you are likely to see numerous Spotted Wobbegongs and Australian Bluespotted Maskrays, and at times they are joined by other stingray and wobbegong species. This is also a good spot to see a variety of grubfish, flatheads, goatfish, scorpionfish and rabbitfish. However, a close inspection of the algae, weed and coral might also reveal Robust Ghostpipefish, frogfish and a variety of blennies, threefins and gobies.

On one dive I even found a Great Seahorse clinging to a sponge – the only one

Bentstick Pipefish (*Trachyrhamphus bicoarctatus*).

I have ever seen. This wide-ranging seahorse can turn up just about anywhere along the east coast. Like all seahorses, the male gets pregnant, with the female depositing her eggs into a special brooding pouch in the male's stomach. He then carries the young for several weeks, with his belly swelling, until they are ready to be born and fend for themselves. The Great Seahorse is only thought to live for two to four years – such a short life for such a beautiful fish.

Beyond the rocky outcrops is a large rocky ridge that is home to a good variety of fishes. Here you will see butterflyfish, wrasses, hawkfish, bullseyes and numerous wobbegongs. A search of the ledges and crevices might also reveal a very rare Colclough's Shark. Only found off southern Queensland and northern New South Wales, this endemic shark is shy and easily overlooked, as they like to hide to avoid being eaten by wobbegongs!

The most popular area at the Northern Ledges is the boulder wall. The base of this wall is a good spot to see wobbegongs, Eastern Blue Groper, sweetlips, morwongs, leatherjackets and schools of stripeys and bullseyes. Australian Pineapplefish are sometimes found sheltering in darker recesses. At the base of the wall Blotched Fantail Stingrays often rest, and during summer Whitespotted Wedgefish and Leopard Shark laze here.

This wall is also a habitat for Bentstick Pipefish. These long thin pipefish can

Colclough's Shark (*Brachaelurus colcloughi*).

Great Seahorse (*Hippocampus kelloggi*).

grow to 40cm in length, and looking like a stick they are easily overlooked. This wide-ranging species is found throughout the tropics to warm temperate seas, living in sheltered bays and estuary habitats and feeding on small crustaceans and zooplankton.

The top of the boulder wall is shallow enough for snorkellers to explore and see a good variety of reef fish and turtles. Common here are butterflyfish, wrasses, surgeonfish, bream, porcupinefish and pufferfish. My favourites here are the Leopard Blennies, which eat coral polyps and are always fun to watch as they dart between the rocks and corals.

41 NINE MILE REEF, TWEED HEADS

Dozens of hidden reefs off the coast of Tweed Heads offer brilliant diving. All have a good population of fishes, with the best in the area located nine miles off the coast, so this site is naturally called Nine Mile Reef.

The main feature of this site is a blade of rock rising from 25m to 12m, that is surrounded by rocky ridges and gutters. This reef is almost constantly washed by current, meaning that corals flourish, but it is not a dive for inexperienced divers. These currents also bring in a good variety of pelagic fish, including schools of Yellowtail Kingfish, bonito, mackerel, barracuda and trevally.

Nine Mile Reef has always been known as a sharky dive, and when first dived in the 1950s was reported to be a good spot to see Shortfin Mako and Bronze Whaler Sharks. Unfortunately, shark nets were installed on the local beaches in 1962 and they quickly wiped out these sharks. However, several shark species can still be seen.

Year-round divers will see Ornate, Spotted and Banded Wobbegongs at Nine

Greater Bamboo Shark (*Chiloscyllium magnus*).

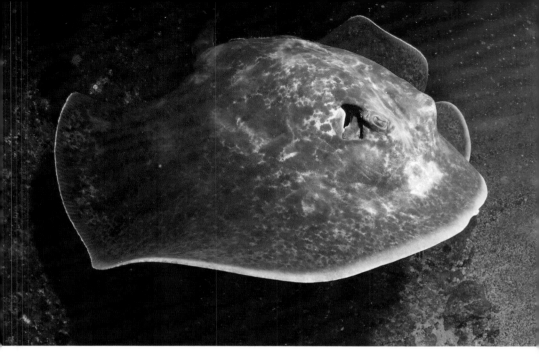

Blotched Fantail Stingray (*Taeniurops meyeni*).

Mile Reef. Summer sees Leopard Sharks visiting, with dozens often observed resting on the sand in the main gutter, and winter brings dozens of Grey Nurse Sharks on their annual migration. If you search the many ledges at this site, you are also likely to find Greater Bamboo Sharks. This species and the Colclough's Shark are easily confused, but they have different fin shapes. The bamboo shark is more common and larger, growing to more than 1.3m in length; this species was only recently described, as it was confused with the wide-ranging Brown-banded Bamboo Shark.

Rays are often seen at Nine Mile Reef. Spotted Eagle Rays glide around the reef and Australian Bluespotted Maskrays feed in the sand. During summer large Whitespotted Wedgefish visit the reef, while schools of Australian Cownose Rays can swim past at any time. The most common ray seen here is Blotched Fantail Stingray – a tropical species that also ventures into subtropical waters. These get quite large, up to 1.8m wide, and the blotched colour pattern can vary from basic black, to black with grey blotches, or grey with black blotches. Pregnant females are seen in late summer, with two huge bulges in their back loaded with up to seven young.

Common Lionfish (*Pterois volitans*) eating a Banded Boxer Shrimp.

While the larger fishes get most of the attention at Nine Mile Reef, this site is also home to a good variety of reef fishes. Common are butterflyfish, angelfish, morays, wrasses, surgeonfish, fusiliers, basslets, hawkfish, morwongs, sweetlips, scorpionfish, pufferfish and boxfish.

The very flamboyant Common Lionfish is often seen at Nine Mile Reef. These fish look spectacular with their feather-like fins, with each tipped with a venomous spine. The Common Lionfish is found throughout the Indo-Pacific region in both tropical and subtropical waters. They are very fierce predators, eating fish and crustaceans, and have even become a pest on reefs in the Western Atlantic after being released there.

42 JULIAN ROCKS, BYRON BAY

Julian Rocks, or Nguthungulli as it is known to the local Arakwal Aboriginal people, is one of the best places to encounter sharks and rays in Australia. While Grey Nurse Sharks in winter and Leopard Sharks and Reef Manta Rays in summer have made the spot famous, the main elasmobranchs seen here are wobbegongs – hundreds of wobbies. So many wobbegongs that I like to call the site Wobby Rocks!

Located off Main Beach at Byron Bay, Julian Rocks is fully protected as a marine reserve. Around the rock are gutters, walls and a lovely cave, in depths from 6m to 26m. Julian Rocks is small enough that you can almost circumnavigate it on one dive. However, it is much better to take your time and slowly explore this fabulous dive site and admire all the fishes.

Wobbegongs are everywhere at Julian Rocks. They pack into caves and ledges, rest on ridges and jam together in the gutters. Dozens of Ornate and Banded

Spotted Wobbegong (*Orectolobus maculatus*).

Wobbegongs can be seen, but they are easily outnumbered by the Spotted Wobbegongs. This species grows to 1.8m in length and is the most social of all the wobbies. Researchers discovered that groups of these sharks rest together, and nearly always with the same individuals. Why they do this is unknown, as it appears to have nothing to do with sex or food. The Spotted Wobbegong is endemic to Australia and found throughout temperate and subtropical zones.

Another species seen in large numbers at Julian Rocks is the Australian Bluespotted Maskray. This species was only recently described and little is known about it or its range. While several are seen on every dive at Julian Rocks, hundreds gather in the gutters in late January for some unknown reason. It is quite a sight to see so many of these rays resting together or swimming around en masse. Most appear to be females, but they are not pregnant or display mating scars, so why they gather here is a complete mystery.

Other sharks and rays found at Julian Rocks include Grey Nurse Shark, Leopard Shark, Blind Shark, Colclough's Shark, Greater Bamboo Shark, Reef Manta Ray, Whitespotted Wedgefish, Spotted Eagle Ray, Blotched Fantail Stingray and schools of Australian Cownose Ray.

Australian Bluespotted Maskray (*Neotrygon australiae*).

Blacksaddle Toby (*Canthigaster valentini*).

Both reef and pelagic fish are seen at Julian Rocks, with barracuda, Mulloway, sweetlips, trevally, mackerel, batfish, morays, coral snapper, morwongs, angelfish, butterflyfish, wrasses, goatfish, surgeonfish and scorpionfish common. Many temperate fishes are regularly seen, including Eastern Blue Groper, Old Wife and Eastern Smooth Boxfish. However, I have also encountered unusual species such as Red Indian Fish and Giant Boarfish.

Julian Rocks is also a good spot to see the cute Blacksaddle Toby. These lovely little fish are often seen in pairs or small groups, slowly moving over the reef in search of food, which can include everything from algae to small invertebrates. A member of the pufferfish family, this species has poisonous flesh, so is ignored by predators. Taking advantage of this, the Blacksaddle Filefish, a type of leatherjacket, has copied its colour pattern, providing this mimic with protection from predators.

43 FISH SOUP, NORTH WEST ROCK, MULLAWAY

With a name like Fish Soup you can understand why this site is included in this list. This is a dive site at North West Rock – one of the many rocky outcrops of the Solitary Islands. These fabulous islands are a marine park and spread over 50km of coastline. They are split into two regions, with the northern group explored from Mullaway or Wooli and the southern group via Coffs Harbour.

North West Rock is a barren outcrop, home to a few seabirds. However, underwater it swarms with fishes. Most dives start on the sheltered western side of the rock, although the best fishes are seen in the gutter that splits the rock in two. Depths at Fish Soup vary from 9m to 20m.

Schooling fish are a feature of this site, with vast numbers of Red Morwong, Yellowback False Fusiliers, Tarwhine, Yellowtail Scad, Australian Mado and Blacktip Bullseyes to be seen. Groups of pretty Orange Basslets, and the rarer Painted Basslets, also reside at this site. Another fish seen in large numbers is the Indo-Pacific Sergeant Major. These damsels lay their eggs on the rocks and they are often eaten by gangs of cheeky Green Moon Wrasse.

Green Moon Wrasse (*Thalassoma lutescens*).

Citron Butterflyfish (*Chaetodon citrinellus*).

These nasty fish are found throughout the tropics and appear to be more abundant on subtropical reefs. Green Moon Wrasse normally eat tiny invertebrates and are mostly seen in small groups. However, when damsels are nesting, they form into large roaming packs so they can overwhelm the poor parents with numbers.

Other common reef fish seen at Fish Soup include Eastern Blue Groper, Pacific Trumpetfish, Yellow Boxfish, Stout Moray and a variety of wrasses, hawkfish, damsels, sweetlips, surgeonfish, goatfish, rockcods and butterflyfish. A lovely butterflyfish seen here is the Citron Butterflyfish. These cute little fish are always seen in pairs, and if they get separated it is nice to watch them either waiting for their partner to catch up, or backtracking to see what has happened to them. They move slowly over the reef, feeding on small invertebrates and coral polyps.

At Fish Soup you will also see wobbegongs, stingrays and maybe a Spotted Eagle Ray or a Grey Nurse Shark. I often look in the nooks and crannies for hiding fish, and have spotted Leopard Blenny, Pacific Rockcod and a number of gobies and threefins.

The rarest fish I have seen here is the Splendid Hawkfish. This wonderfully pattern fish is larger than the average hawkfish, growing to 20cm in length, and is endemic to northern New South Wales, although the odd one turns up in southern Queensland. To get a photo of this rare fish I ended up following it across the reef. It would settle on the bottom, I would sneak up, and just when I got within camera range it would relocate to another spot. It finally realised that I wasn't going to eat it, allowing me to get close enough for a few quick photos.

Splendid Hawkfish (*Notocirrhitus splendens*).

44 THE CANYONS, NORTH SOLITARY ISLAND, MULLAWAY

North Solitary Island is surrounded by many wonderful dive sites. If conditions allow, a dive off the eastern side of the island is spectacular with rock walls and lots of pelagic action. While at the northern end of the island is the sheltered Anemone Bay, where the bottom is carpeted with sea anemones that are home to numerous anemonefish. However, the best spots for fishwatching are on the western side of the island, with The Canyons a favourite.

The Canyons is a series of rocky gutters, ledges and walls in depths from 5 to 24m. A good variety of hard and soft corals decorate the reef, and sea anemones cover the bottom in places, populated with either Barrier Reef and Wideband Anemonefish.

Spotted and Banded Wobbegongs are often observed resting in the gutters, and the occasional Leopard Shark or Grey Nurse Shark can be spotted, depending on the season. The Canyons are also visited by pelagic fishes, so watch for Yellowtail

Australian Sawtail (*Prionurus microlepidotus*).

Crimson Soldierfish (*Myripristis murdjan*).

Kingfish, trevally, mackerel, jobfish and Spotted Eagle Ray. You are also likely to be harassed by several Eastern Blue Gropers as you explore the reef.

Vast schools of Blacktip Bullseyes can cover the reef, and groups of goatfish, fusiliers, bream and Silver Sweep can also be seen. This is also a good spot to see shoals of Australian Sawtails. The sawtails are a member of the surgeonfish family, and have a series of sharp blades at the base of their tail. The Australian Sawtail is only found off the east coast of Australia and grows to 50cm in length. They are mostly seen in schools slowly moving across the bottom, grazing on algae or plankton.

A great assortment of reef fishes are seen at The Canyons, including a good variety of wrasses, butterflyfish, angelfish, damsels, goatfish, hawkfish, parrotfish, rockcods, morwongs, sweetlips, lionfish, scorpionfish, porcupinefish, boxfish, basslets and pufferfish. Some unusual reef fish to look for include Herald's Angelfish, Flame Hawkfish, Thornback Cowfish and Reticulated Butterflyfish.

The many ledges at The Canyons provide shelter for a range of cardinalfish and scorpionfish, as well as Coral Rockcod. A number of these ledges are also filled with Crimson Soldierfish. Soldierfish are nocturnal, so spend the day hiding in dark caves and under ledges. They emerge at night and slowly move across the reef feeding on zooplankton. The Crimson Soldierfish is a wide-ranging species, found around Australia in tropical and subtropical waters, and grows to 25cm in length.

While exploring the many ledges at this site also keep an eye out for morays. White-eyed, Green and even the rare Yellowmouth Moray can be seen, with the most common species being the Stout Moray. This moray is found throughout the Indo-Pacific region and is abundant in this subtropical region of eastern Australia. The Stout Moray grows to 60cm long and feeds on small fish, mostly at night.

Stout Moray (*Gymnothorax eurostus*).

BOULDER WALL, SOUTH SOLITARY ISLAND, COFFS HARBOUR

South Solitary Island is the largest island of the group and accessible from Coffs Harbour. The island has a lighthouse, which at one time was maintained by a lighthouse keeper, but today the only residents of the island are seabirds. Diving around South Solitary Island is spectacular, with walls, caves and rocky reefs to explore, with my favourite for fishwatching being Boulder Wall, on the western side of the island.

Boulder Wall varies in depth from 6m to 25m, with the boulders forming caves, ledges and crevices. This site is a great spot to see pelagic fishes – look out for Yellowtail Kingfish, trevally, batfish, mackerel and Mulloway. Also seen here are Grey Nurse Shark, Spotted, Banded and Ornate Wobbegongs, Blotched Fantail Stingray and the occasionally Coffin Ray.

A number of anemonefish species are found, including the local endemic species, the Wideband Anemonefish. These pretty fish are only found in a small area off southern Queensland and northern New South Wales. The female Wideband Anemonefish lays eggs year-round, that are attended by her male partner. However, a study found that they have more frequent clutches during summer, sometimes

Comb Wrasse (*Coris picta*).

Wideband Anemonefish (*Amphiprion latezonatus*).

three per month. If you find a Wideband Anemonefish, have a close look on the rocks around the anemone as you may also see their precious eggs.

One of the most impressive things about Boulder Wall is the schools of resident reef fish, including Red Morwong, Blacktip Bullseye, Yellowfin Bream, Australian Mado and stripeys. Schools of Yellowstripe Goatfish are common, and unexpectedly so are schools of Blacksaddle Goatfish. This species is one of the largest goatfish, growing to 50cm long. They are found in subtropical regions off both coasts. Juvenile Blacksaddle Goatfish are known to form large schools, although it is unusual to see adults in any gathering larger than a small group.

A great variety of reef fish can be seen on Boulder Wall, including species of butterflyfish, angelfish, surgeonfish, grubfish, damsels, hawkfish, morays, soldierfish,

Blacksaddle Goatfish (*Parupeneus spilurus*).

parrotfish, porcupinefish, pufferfish and sweetlips. The wrasse family is also well represented, with a good number of Eastern Blue Gropers and an interesting mix of small tropical and temperate wrasses. One of these is the Comb Wrasse, which is endemic to New South Wales and southern Queensland. This very distinctive fish has a white body with either a black comb pattern on the male or a black stripe on the juvenile and female. When breeding the male changes colour to grey, almost like the black and white colours have mixed. Comb Wrasses are always busy flitting across the reef in search of small invertebrates to eat.

46 FISH ROCK, SOUTH WEST ROCKS

South West Rocks is one of the most popular dive destinations in New South Wales, as offshore are three islands surrounded by wonderful subtropical rocky reefs. However, the main attraction is a spectacular sea cave that runs right through the middle of Fish Rock.

Fish Rock Cave is 125m long and a mind-blowing dive. The deep end of the cave starts in a gutter at 24m and is quite dark and narrow, while at the other end is a large chamber only 12m deep. The cave is a brilliant dive, however it is the fish life that makes this site extra special.

Inside the cave are schools of Blacktip Bullseye and Eastern Pomfred, and they can be so dense at the entrance that they block out the light. Also commonly seen are Crimson Soldierfish, Blotched Bigeye, Common Lionfish, Eastern Red Scorpionfish and the elusive Pacific Rockcod. Rare Black Rockcod are also found in the cave, although most are camera shy.

Grey Nurse Sharks are a feature of diving Fish Rock, and they are seen year-round, inside and outside the cave. Also found in the cave are Blotched Fantail

Banded Wobbegong (*Orectolobus halei*).

Lyretail Hawkfish (*Cyprinocirrhites polyactis*).

Stingray and Spotted Wobbegong, although these are outnumbered by the larger Banded Wobbegong. This is the largest member of the wobbegong family, growing to 3.2m long. Some are so big they have a head that is one metre wide! The Banded Wobbegong is a temperate species, endemic to southern Australia, yet it is more abundant in subtropical regions. These wobbegongs are quite docile, but they do have a mouthful of long sharp teeth and have bitten many a diver that has annoyed them. The best advice is not to touch or poke them!

While the cave is a fun dive, the rocky reef around Fish Rock is home to even more fishes. Pelagic fish constantly swirl around. Expect to see Longfin Batfish, Yellowtail Kingfish, Pickhandle Barracuda, Silver Trevally and mackerel. Spotted Eagle Rays and Blotched Fantail Stingrays cruise with the currents, and are sometimes joined by schools of Australian Cownose Rays. Something really special happens in spring, when schools of Scalloped Hammerheads appear.

A great variety of reef fish are found. Commonly seen are Eastern Blue Groper, morwongs, leatherjackets, butterflyfish, angelfish, fusiliers, wrasses, damsels, anemonefish, scorpionfish, sweetlips, pufferfish and triggerfish. One of my favourites here are the Lyretail Hawkfish. These hawkfish are only found on reefs exposed to currents, and though a tropical species they are mostly seen in subtropical waters. Like other hawkfish they sit on the bottom and they feed in the water column, darting up and down to grab zooplankton.

Many cracks and crevices cut the rocky reef at Fish Rock. These provide a home for Blind Shark, Ornate Wobbegong, Zebra Lionfish and juvenile Yellow Boxfish. This is also a great spot for morays, including White-eyed and Stout Morays and the rare Mosaic Moray. This last species is one of the most spectacular members of the family, with a mouth overloaded with sharp teeth and an intricate mosaic pattern. The Mosaic Moray grows to 1.8m long and is only found off northern New South Wales and northern New Zealand.

Mosaic Moray (*Enchelycore ramosa*).

47 GREEN ISLAND, SOUTH WEST ROCKS

Fish Rock maybe the most popular dive site off South West Rocks, but nearby is another wonderful site called Green Island. This island is separated from the mainland by a narrow channel, so it is closer to shore and doesn't always have the best visibility. However, it is a more sheltered site than Fish Rock, and gets its own brilliant collection of fishes.

Around Green Island are rocky reefs in depths from 6m to 18m. This reef is riddled with many ledges, gutters and crevices, and beyond the reef is a sandy plain. Spotted and Ornate Wobbegongs are regularly encountered, and quite a few Blind Sharks also shelter in the many recesses. On the sand look for Common Stingaree, Coffin Ray, Australian Bluespotted Maskray and Blotched Fantail Stingray. Whitespotted Wedgefish are sometimes seen during summer.

A search of the sand might reveal an elusive Eastern Shovelnose Ray – a member

Eastern Shovelnose Ray (*Aptychotrema rostrata*).

Starry Pufferfish (*Arothron stellatus*).

of the banjo ray family that is endemic to the east coast of Australia. They are mostly seen in New South Wales, although some turn up at sites in southern Queensland. The Eastern Shovelnose Ray reaches a length of 1.2m and spends the day hidden under a layer of sand. They feed at night, and are known as suction-crushing feeders, digging in the sand with their mouth and sucking up small fish, crustaceans and molluscs, which they crush with their blunt teeth.

Pelagic fish also visit Green Island as the reef is almost constantly swarmed by schools of Yellowtail Scad, Australian Mado, Silver Sweep and Diamondfish. The Diamondfish has many common names, although this one best suits its shape and shiny-sparkly finish. It is closely related to the pomfreds, and is nearly always found in schools in shallow water. This is a wide-ranging species in the Indo-Pacific region, and I have always found it to be more common in subtropical areas, possibly because it favours estuaries in the tropics. They feed on plankton, and are also happy to scavenge sea jellies and dead fish.

Diamondfish (*Monodactylus argenteus*) eating a seajelly.

The rocky reef at Green Island supports a great range of reef fishes. Commonly seen are Tomato Rockcod, Clown Wrasse, Old Wife, Dwarf Hawkfish, Girdled Scalyfin, Red Morwong, Eastern Blue Groper and a variety of butterflyfish, angelfish, damsels, leatherjackets and sweetlips.

Many pufferfish call this site home, including a few large Starry Pufferfish. These can grow to more than 1.2m long and are quite active by day as they feed on small invertebrates, coral polyps, sponges and even algae. The Starry Pufferfish only has four teeth, which are well designed to crush shells and scrape algae. Although a tropical species, it is often found in subtropical waters. They are an easy fish to closely observe, as they are slow swimmers and often ignore divers.

48 LATITUDE ROCK, FORSTER/TUNCURRY

Diving and snorkelling off the twin towns of Forster and Tuncurry is fascinating as it is a transition zone from subtropical to temperate. Little hard coral is seen on the area's rocky reefs – instead sponges, sea tulips and kelp dominate these reefs. This change in habitat also sees a change in fish life, with temperate species outnumbering the tropical species.

Numerous rocky reefs offer exceptional diving off Forster/Tuncurry, with one of the best spots for fishwatching being Latitude Rock. This blade of rock breaks the surface and is surrounded by interesting terrain in depths from 6m to 18m.

Several gutters run through the site and these are the best place to see Grey Nurse Sharks. They swim slow circuits up and down these gutters. However, observing them can be difficult, as they are often obscured by thick schools of Yellowtail Scad, Silver Sweep, Diamondfish and Australian Mado. This last species is endemic to the east coast, and very common in New South Wales. Australian Mado feed on

Eastern Blue Groper (*Achoerodus viridis*).

Halfbanded Seaperch (*Hypoplectrodes maccullochi*).

zooplankton and are often very curious of divers, swarming around them. I have nicknamed them the photographer's nightmare, as they often swim in front of the camera while you are trying to take photos of other more photogenic subjects!

Spotted and Banded Wobbegongs are observed resting in the gutters and ledges at Latitude Rock, often alongside Port Jackson Sharks. These ledges are also a good spot to see Australian Pineapplefish, Eastern Blue Devil, Green Moray and if lucky a Mosaic Moray.

A very common reef fish seen at Latitude Rock is the Eastern Blue Groper. One of the largest members of the wrasse family, these lovely fish grow to 1.2m long. They are a speciality of New South Wales, where every dive site has its family, although their range includes southern Queensland and north-eastern Victoria. They are quite a cheeky fish, and follow divers around hoping for a free feed. They eat a range of invertebrates, and especially love sea-urchin guts. At some dive sites they are so bossy that they even nudge divers to feed them. Similar to other wrasse, the male has a harem of smaller females. The males are also very territorial, not tolerating another male on their patch, as my wife knows when she was accidental bitten when she got between two arguing males!

Typical reef fish seen include Girdled Scalyfin, Eastern Wirrah, Red Morwong, White-ear, Yellowfin Leatherjacket, Smallscale Bullseye, Onespot Puller, Blacksaddle Goatfish and Threebar Porcupinefish. A good variety of wrasses are also seen, including Comb, Eastern King, Crimsonband and Southern Maori Wrasses.

A lovely small reef fish to look for is the Halfbanded Seaperch. These pretty little fish are endemic to the east coast, and mainly seen off New South Wales. They are a small member of the groper family that like to perch on rocks and sponges, keeping an eye out for a possible meal. Halfbanded Seaperch make good photography subjects as their curious nature allows a close approach.

Australian Mado (*Atypichthys strigatus*).

Broughton Island is located north of Port Stephens and protected as a national park. It is an important habitat for nesting seabirds, including Little Penguins, that feed on the rich supply of fishes found around the island. While you have little chance of encountering a penguin underwater, you will see many of the fish they like to dine on.

All around Broughton Island are rocky reefs decorated with sponge gardens and kelp, with one of the best spots to fishwatch being North Rock. The rocky reef at this site varies from 5m to 22m, and has plenty of gutters and boulders to explore.

Thick schools Australian Mado, Sea Sweep, Eastern Pomfred, Diamondfish, Yellowtail Scad, Longfin Pike and Smallscale Bullseye fill the gutters. This last species also populates the ledges and caves; it is endemic to New South Wales and always found in schools. By day these bullseyes mostly shelter in caves, but if there are limited hiding places they also spill across rocky reefs; at night they rise into mid-water to feed on zooplankton.

A few Grey Nurse Sharks are generally spotted in the gutters at North Rock.

Sixspine Leatherjacket (*Meuschenia freycineti*).

Red Morwong (*Morwong fuscus*).

However, divers are more likely to see Banded and Spotted Wobbegongs and Port Jackson Sharks. Smooth Stingrays and Southern Eagle Rays often visit this reef, and I have also spotted an Eastern Shovelnose Stingaree well beyond its normal range.

A very common reef fish is the Red Morwong, which can be seen in abundance in New South Wales, mostly gathered in groups on the bottom. Endemic to the east coast, this species is reported to grow to 65cm, yet fish bigger than 40cm are rarely seen. These thick-lipped fish feed on a range of small invertebrate species, many of which are grabbed with a mouthful of sand. They then filter out the edible critters with gill rakers. Red Morwong spend much of their time sitting on the bottom, which makes them a great subject for underwater photographers.

A wide variety of reef fish are seen at North Rock, either swimming over the reef or hiding among the kelp. Look for Girdled Scalyfin, Eastern Wirrah, Eastern Blue Groper, Old Wife, Eastern Hulafish, Herring Cale, Sergeant Baker, Eastern Red Scorpionfish, Green Moray, Eastern Kelpfish, Bluestriped Goatfish and White-ear. A number of tropical reef fish are also seen here, including Pacific Trumpetfish, Common Lionfish, Longfin Bannerfish and Moorish Idol.

Like most temperate spots in New South Wales, a great assortment of wrasses

Smallscale Bullseye (*Pempheris compressa*).

and leatherjackets can be observed, including some large Sixspine Leatherjackets. This endemic leatherjacket is found throughout Australia's temperate waters and grows to 60cm long. The male is very pretty, with vivid blue stripes and wavy lines, while the female has a more subdued colouration but is still handsome. These fish have a broad diet that includes everything from algae to small invertebrates.

North Rock is also a good spot to look for more unusual temperate fishes hiding under ledges or in the kelp. Divers have seen Eastern Toadfish, Eastern Blue Devil, Yellow Crested Weedfish and Estuary Catfish.

Port Stephens, the blue water wonderland, has some of the best shore diving in Australia. Around the township of Nelson Bay are five wonderful shore-diving sites, However, I have only listed my three favourites for fishwatching. The first is a long stretch of pipe, behind the d'Albora Marina, that is overloaded with fishes.

Like all the shore-diving sites in Port Stephens, The Pipeline is tidal, so best dived on the high tide. The pipe is actually a disused sewer pipe that extends 250m into the bay in depths from 3m to 18m. Sponges, soft corals, ascidians and kelp grow on and around the pipe, and provide a habitat for a wealth of fishes.

While a good variety of reef fish, pelagic fish and small sharks and rays can be seen at The Pipeline, this is a muck site so it's the unusual fish species that are the highlight. A search of the sponge gardens and sand will often reveal Robust Ghostpipefish, White's Seahorse, Bentstick Pipefish and Girdled Pipefish. However, the most common member of the Syngnathidae family seen here is the Tiger Pipefish.

This large endemic pipefish grows to 35cm in length. It is found off both the east and west coasts in subtropical and warm temperate seas, and also surprisingly in the Spencer Gulf in South Australia. Like all pipefish, the male takes on the main role

Male Tiger Pipefish (*Filicampus tigris*) with its eggs exposed.

Striate Frogfish (*Antennarius striatus*) with a nudibranch crawling over it.

in reproduction, carrying the eggs in a pouch on his tail. The eggs are often difficult to see, although I once photographed a male at this site that had his eggs exposed, possibly as a result of an attack from a predator.

Other unusual fish to look for here include Thornback Cowfish, Estuary Catfish, Southern Velvetfish, Spiny Gurnard, Eastern Toadfish, Immaculate Glider Goby and a number of soles. The rare Smooth Frogfish has been spotted at The Pipeline. This strange frogfish keeps its eggs close at hand, attached to its body until they hatch. A more common relative seen here is the Striate Frogfish. Also known as the Hairy Frogfish, because some get long hair-like filaments growing from their body, this species grows to 25cm in length. To aid in camouflage, Striate Frogfish can change their colouration, which takes about five weeks, and can include white, yellow, brown or black. Ambush predators, they sit motionless on the bottom, flicking their worm-like lures to attract fish. The Striate Frogfish is found in tropical to warm temperate waters around Australia, with a strong preference for estuary habitats.

The Pipeline is also a wonderful night dive, with a great range of molluscs and crustaceans emerging to feed. This is the best time to see soles and flounders, and a very secretive eel, the Serpent Eel. This is the most common snake eel seen in Australia and it is found in both temperate and subtropical waters. They are not an easy critter to spot, as they live in the sand and have a sandy colouration. Occasionally a snout is seen protruding by day, however they are far easier to spot at night, when they emerge a little more to grab prey. The Serpent Eel may have a small head, but they can grow to 2.5m in length, although their full length is rarely seen.

Serpent Eel (*Ophisurus serpens*).

51 FLY POINT, PORT STEPHENS

Fly Point, and nearby Halifax Park, are marine reserves and part of the Great Lakes Marine Park. An easy beach entry at Fly Point leads to extensive kelp beds where snorkellers can see a wide variety of temperate reef fishes. However, it is in deeper water where the best fishwatching happens at Fly Point.

Beyond the kelp beds is a series of rocky ledges, in depths from 8m to 24m. These ledges are covered in sponges and soft corals, creating a beautiful tapestry of colours and a fabulous habitat for fishes.

Dense schools of Eastern Pomfred and Blacktip Bullseye swarm over the reef, and are often joined by bream, pike, scad and stripey. The reef fishes at Fly Point are a good mix of tropical species like butterflyfish, angelfish and hawkfish, and temperate species like morwong, leatherjackets and wrasses. Other typical reef

Blind Shark (*Brachaelurus waddi*).

Dusky Flathead (*Platycephalus fuscus*).

fish seen here include tuskfish, triggerfish, surgeonfish, morays, boxfish, pufferfish, scorpionfish, blennies, Old Wife, rockcods, damsels and Eastern Blue Groper.

Fly Point also has an abundance of sharks and rays. Port Jackson Shark, Ornate and Spotted Wobbegong, Common Stingaree and Coffin Ray are all common. However, this is also the best place to see an iconic New South Wales endemic, the Blind Shark. These shy sharks are nocturnal feeders, munching on small fish, crustaceans and squid. By day they like to hide under ledges, to avoid being eaten by wobbegongs. Often all you see of a Blind Shark is a tail hanging out of a hole, yet at Fly Point these cute little sharks sometimes sleep on the sponges, which presumably make a much more comfortable bed. The Blind Shark grows to 1.2m in length and gives birth to live young in spring.

As you go deeper at Fly Point, spend some time investigating the many ledges. These provide shelter for pipefish, cardinalfish, lionfish, Estuary Catfish, Eastern Toadfish, morays and Australian Pineapplefish. Many sand patches are also found at Fly Point, where flounders, soles, grubfish, goatfish and flatheads can be seen.

The most common flathead is the largest member of the family, the Dusky Flathead. Growing to 1.2m in length, some of the ones seen at Fly Point are bigger

Immaculate Glider Goby (*Valenciennea immaculata*).

than the wobbegongs! The females are much longer than the males, and in summer you can often see amorous males snuggling up to much larger females, hoping to get lucky.

Unusual fish observed at Fly Point include frogfish, ghostpipefish, seahorses, cowfish, blennies and gobies. Immaculate Glider Gobies are often seen feeding on the sand in pairs. These attractive fish are considered a tropical and subtropical species, although their range does extend into this temperate zone. They have a lovely metallic sheen, and if you rest quietly on the bottom you can watch them snatching up mouthfuls of sand and filtering it for morsels of food. Unfortunately, if you get too close, they will dart into their burrow in the sand.

52 HALIFAX PARK, PORT STEPHENS

Halifax Park is the third great shore-diving site at Port Stephens and the deepest of the three. The rocky reef here drops to 30m, with lots of walls, ledges, ridges and little caves to explore that play host to a brilliant variety of fishes.

Of the three shore-diving sites, Halifax Park is closer to the ocean and experiences the strongest currents on the change of the tide. This means you are more likely to see ocean-going fishes compared to the estuary fishes seen at Fly Point and The Pipeline. You can often see pelagic fishes such as Yellowtail Kingfish, Silver Trevally, Australasian Snapper and Longfin Pike, while I have also seen Southern Eagle Ray, Australian Bluespotted Maskray and Sergeant Baker at Halifax Park, but not at the other two sites.

Reef fish are abundant at Halifax Park, with Eastern Blue Groper, Old Wife, wobbegongs, stingarees, morwong, wrasses, butterflyfish, surgeonfish, goatfish, boxfish and a good variety of leatherjackets to be seen. A very common species here is the Eastern Red Scorpionfish. One of the largest members of the scorpionfish family, growing to 40cm in length, they maybe camouflaged but they are very hard to miss as they like to sit proudly on top of the toadstool sponges, which doesn't

Eastern Red Scorpionfish (*Scorpaena jacksoniensis*).

Estuary Catfish (*Cnidoglanis macrocephalus*).

really aid camouflage. These scorpionfish can be very long lived, with researchers studying one fish that was 33 years old!

Not as many unusual fishes are seen at Halifax Park – just the occasional Australian Pineapplefish, seahorse or pipefish. However, this is a good spot to see Estuary Catfish. This large catfish, which is also called the Estuary Cobbler, grows to 90cm in length and is mainly found hiding under ledges by day. At night they emerge to feed on just about anything, including fish, invertebrates and algae. Estuary Catfish have venomous spines, and while they are not the most attractive of fish, they are good parents. The female lays her eggs in a cave in spring and summer, and the male then guards them and the young larvae until they are big enough to look after themselves.

Halifax Park is also a good spot to see morays. The Green Moray is the most common species, while the rarer Sawtooth Moray is sometimes seen. Although its range is reported to be throughout New South Wales, Halifax Park is the only place I have observed this species. The Sawtooth grows to 1.5m in length and like other morays it spends the day in a lair, emerging at night to feed on fish, cephalopods and crustaceans.

Recently researchers discovered that morays are the most cosmopolitan of all fishes. This means that there is little genetic difference in most of the widespread species, including species found on either side of the Pacific Ocean. This is because some morays have very long larval stages, years in some species, which allows them to cover vast distances and keep stirring the gene pool. Other species, such as the Sawtooth Moray, appear to have shorter larval stages, which limits their range.

Sawtooth Moray (*Gymnothorax prionodon*).

53 SHELLY BEACH, MANLY, SYDNEY

ydney divers are spoilt for choice when it comes to dive sites. The sandstone coastline here is littered with rocky reefs and shipwrecks that can be explored by boat. However, Sydney is also blessed with many wonderful shore-diving and snorkelling sites, and these are my favourite for fishwatching.

Shelly Beach is a popular spot for dive training and protected as part of the Cabbage Tree Bay Aquatic Reserve. An easy beach entry gives access to a rocky reef on each side of the bay, with depths varying from 4m to 18m, depending on which way you go. Sponges, sea tulips, ascidians, sea anemones and kelp decorate the reef and provide a habitat for an extensive range of fishes.

Sharks and rays are a feature of Shelly Beach. Commonly seen are Spotted Wobbegong, Blind Shark, Common Stingaree, Eastern Fiddler Ray, Smooth Stingray and Port Jackson Shark. Less common are Coffin Ray, Australian Angel Shark and Crested Hornshark. From January to June dozens of juvenile Dusky Whaler Sharks enter the bay, turning the area into a shark nursery. They are best observed when snorkelling, as they are a little shy of divers.

Spotted Grubfish (*Parapercis ramsayi*).

Juvenile Eastern Smooth Boxfish (*Anoplocapros inermis*).

Common reef fish seen off Shelly Beach include Eastern Blue Groper, wrasses, goatfish, morays, morwongs, leatherjackets, Old Wife, Australian Mado, flatheads, damsels and a surprising number of tropical species.

In the middle of the bay are seagrass beds and sandy patches where divers will see Spotted Grubfish. Grubfish are bottom-dwellers that grub in the sand for food. They mostly sit on the bottom, so are easy to approach to observe and photograph. The Spotted Grubfish is endemic to southern Australia and is one of the cuter members of the family, having large eyes and a round head.

A wonderful fish often seen at Shelly Beach is the Eastern Smooth Boxfish. These charming fish often hide in the kelp, so you may have to look for them. Endemic to the temperate waters of the east coast, this species grows to 35cm in length and is usually a pretty yellow colour with darker spots, with mature males having a pale blue colouration. I always like finding the juveniles of this species as they look like a little yellow ball with fins. These boxfish mainly feed at night on small crustaceans.

Eastern Cleaner Clingfish (*Cochleoceps orientalis*).

Many other fishes hide in the kelp and seagrass at Shelly Beach. Look for Snakeskin Wrasse, Rainbow Cale, Eastern Kelpfish and Rosy Weedfish. One busy little fish found on the kelp is the Eastern Cleaner Clingfish, which only grow to 5cm in length but boldly clean other reef fish, leaping onto them to remove parasites and old skin. Observing this behaviour is not easy, as the cleaning stations can be hidden from view. However, a little giveaway is when you find an Eastern Blue Groper lying on the bottom, as they generally don't do this unless they are getting cleaned. The Eastern Cleaner Clingfish is only found off New South Wales.

54 CHOWDER BAY, CLIFTON GARDENS, SYDNEY

There are several dive sites inside Sydney Harbour that are very interesting to explore. This huge harbour has countless bays and headlands, and also many rocky reefs and shipwrecks. However, for those into fishwatching I would recommend a dip at Chowder Bay, in the suburb of Clifton Gardens.

Dominating this bay is an 80m-long jetty and an ocean swimming pool enclosure. Wading in from the beach, divers can explore under the jetty or on the sandy bottom around it. And in depths from 2m to 10m, divers will find a fascinating collection of reef and muck fish.

The reef fish include leatherjackets, morwong, wrasses, porcupinefish, morays, flatheads, soles, scorpionfish, pufferfish, goatfish, bream, Old Wife, butterflyfish and lionfish. Both Ornate and Robust Ghostpipefish turn up here during the summer months.

Bigbelly Seahorse can also make an appearance, although they are easily outnumbered by the White's Seahorse, which is endemic to New South Wales and southern Queensland, with a preference for estuary habitats. The species grows to 13cm in length, and likes to cling to sponges, seagrass and the nets of the pool at this site. Sadly, the White's Seahorse has declined in number over the last few decades, possibly due to habitat loss. I remember diving in the 1980s when you could see dozens on a dive. Now you are lucky to see one or two.

White's Seahorse (*Hippocampus whitei*).

Widebody Pipefish (*Stigmatopora nigra*).   Below: Hoese's Sandgoby (*Istigobius hoesei*).

The sandy bottom at Chowder Bay supports some unique mucky fishes. Striate Frogfish are commonly seen, yet divers have also seen Painted and Freckled Frogfish, Southern and Patchwork Velvetfish, Slender Seamoth, Painted Stinkfish, Oriental Flying Gurnard and Serpent Eel. Several pipefish are seen in Chowder Bay, including Tiger, Girdled and Mother-of-Pearl Pipefish. In the seagrass and algae look for Widebody Pipefish. These little fish are reported to grow to 16cm long, although most are less than 8cm long and hard to spot as they look exactly like a piece of seaweed. Found throughout southern waters, the Widebody Pipefish breeds year-round; they live fast and die young, with a lifespan of only 150 days.

Other unusual fish seen in Chowder Bay include Eastern Toadfish, Australian Pineapplefish, Thornback Cowfish and Estuary Catfish. Blennies and gobies are also well represented, with Brown Sabretooth Blenny, Horned Blenny, Immaculate Glider Goby, Sculptured Goby and Eastern Longfin Goby documented. The most common goby seen here is the Hoese's Sandgoby. From the name it is easy to deduce that these small fish live on the sand, feeding on anything edible they can grab. The Hoese's Sandgoby grows to 10cm in length and is found from southern Queensland to central New South Wales. They are an easy fish to watch as they slowly skip across the sand, never in much of a hurry.

55 BARE ISLAND, LA PEROUSE, SYDNEY

I grew up in Sydney and it was where I learnt to snorkel and dive. During that time my favourite dive site was Bare Island, and even now I revisit this wonderful site every time I'm in Sydney. This is because the rocky reef around the island swarms with reef fish, and it is also home to some very unusual species.

Bare Island sits just inside the entrance to Botany Bay, and located in such a strategic location it had a fort built on it in the 1880s. Today the fort is a tourist attraction. However, for divers it is the extensive rocky reefs around the island that are the main attraction. You can dive either side of the island to find beautiful sponge gardens and many ledges, caves and boulders in depths to 25m. I generally start by diving the deeper reef off the south-western side of the island and finish on the shallow rocky wall on the eastern side.

This deep reef is the best spot to see a very strange fish, the Red Indian Fish. This

Sydney Pygmy Pipehorse (*Idiotropiscis lumnitzeri*).

bizarre endemic species is found off both the east and west coasts, with Bare Island the most consistent spot to find one. Looking like a sponge, this fish is an ambush predator, using its camouflage to feed on small crustaceans. They don't like to move much, and when they do they rock back and forth like they are a piece of broken sponge. Although Red Indian Fish grow to 27cm in length they are not easy to find, especially if sitting among similar coloured sponges.

The rocky reef at Bare Island supports a great variety of reef fishes. Typically seen are Eastern Blue Groper, White-ear, Sergeant Baker, Common Stingaree, Eastern Red Scorpionfish, Old Wife, Red Morwong, Green Moray and a good variety of wrasses and leatherjackets. Less commonly encountered are Port Jackson Shark, Spotted Wobbegong, Bigbelly Seahorse, Eastern Blue Devil, Eastern Toadfish, Australian Pineapplefish and an assortment of pipefish and weedfish.

Spiny Gurnard (*Lepidotrigla papilio*).

Red Indian Fish (*Pataecus fronto*).

One fish I always look for, and don't always find, is the spectacular Spiny Gurnard. This pretty fish is found in temperate waters throughout Australia, and varies in colour depending on where you see it. Off New South Wales they are typically reddish with bright blue pectoral fins, while the ones off Victoria are light brown with pale blue pectoral fins. This gurnard is a bottom-dwelling fish that walks across the sand using finger-like fins. Its colourful pectoral fins are usually hidden, and only opened as a vivid display when threatened, typically when a diver gets too close.

Many unusual small fishes are found hiding at Bare Island. Eastern Cleaner Clingfish, Lance Blenny, Ringscale Threefin and Horned Blenny can be located with a little effort. Also keep an eye out for frogfish, ghostpipefish and soles. However, the prize fish to find here is the Sydney Pygmy Pipehorse. Only growing to 6cm in length, and extremely well camouflaged, finding one of these strange fish in the algae is quite a challenge. Discovered in 1997 by a very observant Sydney diver, the Sydney Pygmy Pipehorse is only found off Sydney and the south coast. They have a strong site fidelity, and have been recorded staying on the same patch of algae for more than eight months. Bare Island is the best place to see one of these amazing little fish, and I have sometimes found four grouped together on one clump of algae.

56 SUTHERLAND POINT, KURNELL, SYDNEY

Located only one kilometre from Bare Island, directly across Botany Bay, you would think that Sutherland Point would have the exact same fishes. To some extent it does, just in different numbers, as some fishes that are rarely seen at Bare Island are common at Sutherland Point and vice versa. This may be because Sutherland Point is more tidal and washed by currents.

Sutherland Point, along with Inscription Point, form the southern headland of Botany Bay. This entire headland is protected as part of the Kamay Botany Bay National Park, meaning you have to pay an entry fee to enter. Diving is possible at both Inscription Point and Sutherland Point, with Sutherland Point having a greater range of habitats, so more fishes.

This isn't the easiest shore dive in Sydney, requiring a walk down a narrow path

Southern Pygmy Leatherjacket (*Brachaluteres jacksonianus*).

Red-fingered Frogfish (*Porophryne erythrodactylus*).

on the cliff face. And if a swell is hitting the shore forget it. In calm conditions you can safely enter to explore a rocky reef in depths to 18m. There are numerous habitats to explore: kelp beds, sponge gardens, rocky caves and ledges, and some mucky spots as you travel further into the bay. The reef fishes are similar to Bare Island, with more pelagic fish seen, such as Yellowtail Kingfish and Silver Trevally.

A gorgeous little reef fish to look for here is the tiny Southern Pygmy Leatherjacket. Growing to only 10cm long, these little fish are found throughout the temperate waters of Australia. They come in a range of colours – yellow, green, orange or brown – and are very photogenic. They are slow swimmers and easy to observe, and at night they bite onto a piece of seaweed to avoid being swept away.

This is one of the best spots in Sydney to see Weedy Seadragon. These wonderful fish use to be very common here, and in the 1980s you could see a dozen on a dive. Sadly, their numbers seem to have declined. Divers are more likely to see their cousins, Bigbelly Seahorses and the recently described Red Wide-bodied Pipefish. Growing to around 20cm long, these red coloured pipefish like to hide in similarly coloured algae and finger sponges, making them difficult to find.

Other unusual fish to look for at Sutherland Point include Sydney Pygmy Pipehorse, Australian Pipeapplefish, Southern Velvetfish, Painted Stinkfish and Eastern Toadfish. A very special fish seen at this site is the Red-fingered Frogfish. This well-camouflaged fish is only found from Sydney to Jervis Bay, with Botany Bay the best place to see one. Like all frogfish, this species has a head lure to attract prey. The only problem is finding one, as their skin colouration and texture looks exactly like the surrounding sponges.

This site also has numerous ledges where wobbegongs, Port Jackson Shark, bullseyes, Largetooth Beardie and Green Moray like to hide. Under many of these ledges are also groups of Sydney Cardinalfish. These small endemic fish are found throughout New South Wales and into southern Queensland; growing to 14cm in length, they are quite pretty with their bold stripes and pink fins.

Sydney Cardinalfish (*Ostorhinchus limenus*).

SHIPROCK, LILLI PILLI, SYDNEY

Hidden in Port Hacking is a wonderful dive site called Shiprock. This tidal site features a rocky wall covered in spectacular sponges, soft corals and ascidians, and is the perfect habitat for an incredible range of fishes. It is so special that it has been designated as an aquatic reserve.

Located at the end of Shiprock Road, where parking can be a challenge on weekends, to access Shiprock you walk down a pathway between two houses. An easy entry leads to a sandy beach that slopes to 5m, where a wall then drops to 15m. This wall is undercut with ledges and a great place to see the very strange Eastern Toadfish.

Possessing a face that only a mother could love, the Eastern Toadfish spends much of its life hidden under ledges, with only its bearded face showing. They grow to 35cm in length and are ambush predators, feeding on almost anything that comes close to their lair. To aid in the consumption of large prey their stomachs

Eastern Toadfish (*Batrachomoeus dubius*).

Australian Pineapplefish (*Cleidopus gloriamaris*).

can expand considerably. This endemic species is found off New South Wales and southern Queensland, with a preference for estuary habitats, with Shiprock a great place to see one or two.

Exploring the colourful wall at Shiprock, divers will see a good variety of leatherjackets, morwong, wrasses, cardinalfish, blennies, goatfish, damsels, flatheads and scorpionfish. Coffin Ray, Spotted Wobbegong, Green Moray and Eastern Smooth Boxfish are commonly seen, and if you are lucky you may encounter a Crested Hornshark, Southern Eagle Ray or Eastern Fiddler Ray.

Several unusual fishes are found at Shiprock, including species of pipefish, frogfish and seahorses. A surprising number of tropical fishes also populate the site, including butterflyfish, surgeonfish and triggerfish.

Shiprock is also a great place to see the very bizarre Australian Pineapplefish. These strange fish have a ridged exoskeleton with a pattern that looks exactly like a pineapple. Growing to 25cm in length, they spend most of the day hiding under ledges, emerging at night to feed on small crustaceans. To aid them in this task they have bioluminescent organs below the eyes that glow in the dark and attract unsuspecting prey. Often found in small groups, the Australian Pineapplefish is found off both the east and west coasts of Australia.

Many small fishes shelter at Shiprock, either in the sand, among the sponges, or under the many ledges. Keep an eye out for Eastern Fortescue, Ringscale Threefin, Eastern Hulafish, Lyretail Dartgoby and Crested Oystergoby. A pretty little fish often seen here is the Threadfin Reefgoby. This is actually a tropical species, yet I have never seen one on a coral reef, only in estuaries off New South Wales. They grow to 4cm long and are best seen hiding under ledges or among seaweed, especially in the shallows. They are generally found in male/female pairs, and laboratory experiments found that both males and females can change sex if required, due to the loss of a partner.

Threadfin Reefgoby (*Priolepis nuchifasciata*).

58 BLUE METAL LOADER, BASS POINT

The South Coast of New South Wales offers the diver and snorkeller brilliant underwater experiences on temperate rocky reefs. Many of these reefs are only accessible by boat. However, this area also has a number of remarkable shore-diving sites, which are also known as rock hops as most have entries over rocks.

Bass Point is a peninsula near Shellharbour, and the site of a blue metal quarry. There are more than a dozen great dive sites around Bass Point, with my favourite for fishwatching being an artificial structure, the Blue Metal Loader. Built in 1973 to replace an older loader, the structure sits on a rocky reef in depths from 6m to 12m. As long as there isn't a ship being loaded, you can dive the Blue Metal Loader at any time.

The pylons and rocky reef under the loader form a great habitat for reef fishes. Commonly seen are a good variety of wrasses, leatherjackets, damsels, morwongs, flatheads, bullseyes and goatfish.

Old Wife (*Enoplosus armatus*).

Sergeant Baker (*Latropiscis purpurissatus*).

A very common species seen here is the Old Wife, which is found throughout the temperate waters of southern Australia and often seen in large schools. It was one of the first fishes described by Europeans in 1790. This pretty black-and-white fish was classified as a type of butterflyfish, but more recent studies have placed it in its own family. Under the Blue Metal Loader it is hard to avoid Old Wives as schools of several hundred mill around the kelp and pylons.

Other fish seen in schools at this site include Australian Mado, Longfin Pike, Yellowtail Scad, Eastern Pomfred and Yellowtail Kingfish. Exploring the rocky reef, divers also have a good chance of seeing Smooth Stingray, Eastern Fiddler Ray, Crested Hornshark, Green Moray and Eastern Blue Groper. Even Grey Nurse Sharks sometimes make a surprise appearance under the loader.

A large fish often seen sitting on the rocks is the Sergeant Baker. This attractive endemic species grows to 60cm in length and is found throughout southern Australia; it is an ambush predator that waits quietly on the bottom for potential prey to get close, which can include crustaceans, molluscs and small fish.

Eastern Kelpfish (*Chironemus marmoratus*).

Many ledges and crevices cut into the rocky reef under the Blue Metal Loader, and these provide a home for Eastern Toadfish, Sydney Cardinalfish, Horned Blenny, Eastern Blue Devil and Largetooth Beardie. The seagrass, kelp and sand adjacent to the reef is also worth a look as more cryptic and unusual fishes hide here. In these areas I have seen juvenile Weedy Seadragon, pipefish, Eastern Cleaner Clingfish and even a bizarre Slender Sea Moth.

Two fish to look for in the seagrass are Rock Cale and Eastern Kelpfish. At first glance these two bottom-dwelling fish look very alike; as they have a similar body shape and both have a banded pattern with small white spots. However, the Rock Cale has a blunt head and is a type of seacarp, while the Eastern Kelpfish has a pointed head and is in the kelpfish family. They both grow to 40cm in length and are mostly seen in New South Wales. Of the two, the kelpfish is easier to approach to observe and photograph, often allowing divers to closely inspect them.

59 THE DOCKS, JERVIS BAY

Jervis Bay is a huge body of water, with many lovely beaches and some excellent dive sites. The towering sea cliffs at the entrance to the bay continue underwater to form impressive walls and caves. However, the dive sites inside the headlands have always been my favourite for fishwatching, with The Docks on the northern side of the bay a standout.

The Docks is a series of channels that cut into the rocky cliff, that continue underwater to form caves, ledges and gutters in depths to 22m. The sponge gardens at this site are unbelievable – a colourful collection of sea tulips, sponges and gorgonians. Both reef and pelagic fish are common, including a good variety of leatherjackets, damsels, wrasses and morwongs, alongside Yellowtail Kingfish, Silver Trevally and Yellowtail Scad.

The many caves shelter a great variety of fishes, including Largetooth Beardie, Green Moray, Eastern Red Scorpionfish, Banded Wobbegong, Southern Roughy, Eastern Hulafish and Bigscale Bullseye.

These caves also provide a home for one of the most beautiful fish in New South

Port Jackson Shark (*Heterodontus portusjacksoni*).

Eastern Blue Devil (*Paraplesiops bleekeri*).

Wales, the Eastern Blue Devil, which has the most brilliant colour pattern of all the blue devil species found in Australia. These fish grow to 40cm in length, and spend most of the day hidden in caves, often perched on their long pectoral fins. They are more active at night, feeding on brittle stars. The males are reported to be territorial, chasing off other males, the main reason they are found alone. This species is found throughout New South Wales, with the South Coast the best area to see one. The Docks is a reliable location to see two or three of these lovely fish.

A more elusive species found in the caves at The Docks is the Black-banded Seaperch. A number of seaperch are found in the temperate waters of Australia. They are part of the large groper family, with most less than 30cm long. As their name suggests they like to perch, sitting on the bottom on their fins. This species is found throughout New South Wales, yet is rarely seen as it likes to hide in caves. When looking for one, always check the cave ceiling, as they often perch upside-down.

Black-banded Seaperch (*Hypoplectrodes annulatus*).

The sponge gardens at The Docks are also home to Old Wife, Sergeant Baker, Clown Toby and the occasional Red Indian Fish, while the sand is the place to see Smooth Stingray, Kapala Stingaree and Eastern Fiddler Ray.

During winter The Docks, and other sites in Jervis Bay, are overrun with Port Jackson Sharks. This is the largest member of the hornshark family, growing to 1.7m in length. It is found in temperate waters throughout southern Australia, and is an iconic Aussie shark. 'PJs', as they are affectionately known, have small teeth that are used to crush the shells of prey. They can be seen year-round, often hidden in caves, and during winter they gather in the shallows en masse to breed. The females then lay 10 to 16 corkscrew-shaped eggs that are wedged under rocks, with the young sharks hatching around 12 months later. Close encounters with PJs are always fun, as they are sleepy during the day and allow divers to get very close.

60 THE NURSERY, JERVIS BAY

The southern headland of Jervis Bay is formed by Bowen Island. Part of the Booderee National Park, the island is an important breeding site for seabirds, including Little Penguins. Great diving can be experienced right around the island, with my favourite site, The Nursery, on the sheltered western side. You don't see many juvenile fish at this site, so I'm not to sure how it got the name, although you certainly see a good variety of temperate fishes.

The Nursery has a maze of rocky ridges in depths from 8m to 18m. This rocky reef is covered in colourful sponge gardens, kelp and seaweed, and divers can also explore ledges, gutters and a vast plain of sand. This is a great spot to see sharks, including Spotted and Banded Wobbegongs, Port Jackson Shark, Crested Hornshark and the occasional Australian Angel Shark. I haven't seen an angel shark at this site for many years as their numbers have sadly declined. However, I will never forget one encounter here in the 1980s when an open-water student was kneeling on a poor angel shark, completely unaware of its struggles to get free. I pushed the student out of the way and the cranky shark then swam around the students snapping its jaw in protest!

Kapala Stingaree (*Urolophus kapalensis*).

Ocean Leatherjacket (*Nelusetta ayraud*).

The Nursery is an even better spot for rays, with Smooth Stingray, Eastern Fiddler Ray, Southern Eagle Ray and Eastern Shovelnose Ray all common. Another common ray seen here is the Kapala Stingaree. Stingarees are a family of rays that are quite small, with short tails and a varying number of tail barbs. Australian waters are home to the largest variety of stingarees, with 21 species. The Kapala Stingaree is found off New South Wales, mostly on the South Coast, and grows to 50cm in length.

While looking for rays over the sand, don't settle on the bottom or you could end up getting an electric shock from a Coffin Ray. These short chubby rays go by a variety of common names, and anyone who has had a close encounter will never forget it. The Coffin Ray is the most common electric ray in Australia, found off both the east and west coasts. They can generate up to 200 volts by rubbing modified muscles together. They use these electric shocks to stun prey, mainly fish,

Coffin Ray (*Hypnos monopterygius*).

and also for defence, including against divers who touch them! The Coffin Ray is mostly found by accident, as they like to bury in the sand by day, so spotting one can be difficult.

The Nursery has a good population of reef fishes, including Eastern Blue Groper, morwongs, damsels, Old Wife, cardinalfish, Eastern Talma, wrasses and Eastern Blue Devil. Unusual fish seen here include Spiny Gurnard, Bigbelly Seahorse and even a few tropical species, especially during summer.

Leatherjackets are found in large numbers, with Rough, Sixspine, Toothbrush and Yellowstriped Leatherjackets common. The cheekiest member of this family is also encountered here, the Ocean Leatherjacket. This is a wide-ranging temperate species that is mainly found in deep water and can grow to 1m in length. The Ocean Leatherjacket is often seen in schools and is very aggressive towards other fish, biting hunks of flesh out of them. They have also been recorded attacking divers! Fortunately, most of the ones seen on inshore reefs are small, less than 30cm long, and more curious than aggressive.

When I lived in Sydney, a weekend at Ulladulla was always a great escape. Only three hours drive south of the big smoke, the beauty of Ulladulla is that most of its dive sites are close to the harbour, so no long boat rides for those who get seasick. A dozen great boat-diving sites can be explored, including the always-brilliant Lighthouse Wall.

This long blade of rock is located right in front of the lighthouse, and features a rocky wall dropping to 22m and boulders, ledges and gutters. Like all the sites on the South Coast this rocky reef is covered in exquisite sponge gardens, is home to reef fishes and visited by pelagic fishes.

At the base of the wall, where it hits the sand, is a good place to see rays. Kapala Stingaree and Eastern Fiddler Ray are common, but also keep an eye out for Smooth Stingray and Coffin Ray. Port Jackson Sharks gather here in winter, and many can still be seen sheltering under ledges during summer. The resident Eastern Blue Groper will often escort you on a dive, until you enter another groper's territory.

A lovely fish to look for at Lighthouse Wall is the Eastern Talma. This is one of the only temperate butterflyfish, and it is endemic to New South Wales. They are

Eastern Talma (*Chelmonops truncatus*).

Green Moray (*Gymnothorax prasinus*).

actually more common off the Central Coast, although a good number still turn up on the South Coast. The Eastern Talma is generally seen in pairs, with the couple swimming over the reef and picking at small invertebrates they find.

Common reef fishes observed at Lighthouse Wall include Southern Maori Wrasse, Eastern Wirrah, Sergeant Baker, Girdled Scalyfin and Red Morwong. Schools of Old Wife, Australian Mado, Silver Sweep, Onespot Puller and Smallscale Bullseye can also swarm over the reef. Pelagic fishes include schools of Silver Trevally, Luderick, Silver Drummer and Eastern Australian Salmon.

Hiding in ledges at Lighthouse Wall are always a few Green Morays. This eel is Australia's most common temperate moray species, and while its range extends from southern Queensland to central Western Australia, they are mostly seen off New South Wales. They grow to 90cm in length and like all morays they have a reputation for being dangerous and aggressive. In reality they are quite docile if not harassed. However, I wouldn't recommend placing your hand in or near any dark holes, as they have been known to bite wayward fingers.

This is another temperate rocky reef with a good variety of leatherjackets, including the attractive Black Reef Leatherjacket. This endemic leatherjacket ranges throughout Australia's temperate waters, although it is another species that is mainly seen on the New South Wales South Coast. It grows to 40cm in length and is nearly always seen in pairs. They seem to prefer rocky reefs, and are often seen darting in and out of ledges.

Black Reef Leatherjacket (*Eubalichthys bucephalus*).

62 SEAL BAY, MONTAGUE ISLAND, NAROOMA

Montague Island is a spectacular rocky outcrop located 9km off the coast from Narooma. The island is surrounded by rocky reefs, and is most famous among divers for its large colony of Australian Fur Seals. Thousands of fur seals use the island as a resting spot, and diving or snorkelling with them is a fantastic experience. However, Montague Island is also a great place to see fishes.

Mention the word 'seal' and many naturally think of Great White Sharks. While the odd Great White has been seen at Montague Island, the seal colony is actually full of sub-adults and is a non-breeding site, so the sharks don't feed here. The main sharks you will see are Port Jackson Shark, Spotted Wobbegong and Grey Nurse Shark during the summer months.

Seal Bay is a sheltered site on the western side of the island and features boulders, gutters and ledges in depths from 6m to 30m. A common species always seen is the

Smooth Stingray (*Bathytoshia brevicaudata*).

Eastern Fiddler Ray (*Trygonorrhina fasciata*).

Smooth Stingray. Found throughout Australia's temperate waters, this large ray can reach 2m in width and weigh up to 350kg. They are especially common under jetties and near boat ramps, cleaning up the scraps left by anglers. Divers get to know some of these stingrays quite well, seeing them on a regular basis. The ones seen in Seal Bay are often chased by the fur seals, which can be very entertaining to watch.

Other rays are seen at this site, including Eastern Shovelnose Stingaree and Common Stingaree, and I once encountered an Oceanic Manta Ray being followed by a gang of playful fur seals. Another common ray seen at Seal Bay is the Eastern Fiddler Ray. This endemic species is found off New South Wales and occasionally southern Queensland, growing to 1.2m in length and feeding mainly on crustaceans. They sometimes hide under a layer of sand, and at Seal Bay they often shelter under the kelp. You can generally find two or three as you explore the rocky reef.

A good variety of reef fishes can be seen at Seal Bay, including a surprising number of tropicals, as the island is constantly washed by the East Australian Current. Look for Green Moray, Eastern Blue Groper, Old Wife, Moorish Idol, leatherjackets,

Grey Morwong (*Nemadactylus douglasii*).

wrasses, perch, damsels, trevally, Yellowtail Kingfish, snapper, Longsnout Boarfish and even boxfish and cowfish. Three species of morwong are seen here – Red, Banded and Grey Morwongs. The Grey Morwong has been heavily targeted by anglers, so their numbers have been drastically depleted. This species grows to 81cm in length and has a lovely blue-silver sheen. You don't see them often these days, so to encounter one at Seal Bay is a treat.

Montague Island is located close to the continental shelf, so some unexpected pelagic fishes can turn up here. Over the years divers have seen Bluebottle Fish, Shortfin Mako, Bronze Whaler and even Bumphead Sunfish.

63 TATHRA WHARF, TATHRA

Tathra Wharf is a tricky shore dive, as the entry and exit require a little bit of local knowledge. However, once in the water divers can explore a rocky reef in depths from 6m to 12m, which is covered in pretty sponge gardens and home to a good variety of fishes.

Like many spots on the South Coast, this is a good spot to find endemic sharks and rays. Commonly seen are Smooth Stingray, Banded Wobbegong, Port Jackson Shark, Crested Hornshark and Eastern Fiddler Ray. A close inspection of the sponge garden will reveal Bigbelly Seahorses clinging to similar coloured sponges or sea tulips.

A common reef fish seen at Tathra Wharf is the friendly Crimsonband Wrasse, which often follow divers around, hoping that they will uncover some tasty morsel for them to eat. They feed on a range of invertebrates and can often be seen inspecting the bottom for a potential meal. Only the male has a crimson band, while the female is brown with white flecks. Like other wrasse the male has a harem of females, and if he dies the head female changes sex to take his place. This wrasse is found from southern Queensland to Tasmania, and is most common off New South Wales.

Crimsonband Wrasse (*Notolabrus gymnogenis*).

Mosaic Leatherjacket (*Eubalichthys mosaicus*).

Other reef fish commonly encountered here include Eastern Blue Groper, White-ear, Green Moray, Bluestripe Goatfish, Eastern Kelpfish, Longsnout Boarfish, Old Wife, Snakeskin Wrasse, Halfbanded Seaperch, Eastern Smooth Boxfish and morwongs. Leatherjackets are also abundant, including the pretty Mosaic Leatherjacket. This species is found throughout the temperate waters of southern Australia and grows to 60cm in length. Unlike most leatherjackets they have a round body shape and a pretty yellow-and-blue pattern of stripes and blotches. This leatherjacket is a slow swimmer, so easy to observe as it moves among the kelp, sponges and rocks.

Pelagic fishes are also seen at this site, so don't be surprised if a school of Yellowtail

Common Gurnard Perch (*Neosebastes scorpaenoides*).

Kingfish, Longfin Pike or Eastern Australian Salmon surround you. Several unusual fishes are possible if you search the sponge gardens and the many ledges. Divers have seen Australian Pineapplefish, Eastern Talma, Lord Howe Butterflyfish, Rosy Weedfish and Horned Blenny.

Finally, don't forget to check out the sand as you might spot flatheads, soles, flounders and even a Common Gurnard Perch. This strange-looking fish is endemic to the south-east corner of Australia, although mostly seen off Tasmania and Victoria. It grows to 40cm long and is actually a type of scorpionfish, with venomous spines. They are mostly seen sitting on the bottom by day, then venture over the sand and reef at night to feed.

The southernmost section of the New South Wales coast is affectionately called the Sapphire Coast because of the wonderful blue waters that lap the beaches here. And with blue water comes great snorkelling and diving.

Offshore from Merimbula and nearby Eden are rocky reefs covered in pretty sponge gardens and a few shipwrecks to explore. All these sites have great temperate fish life, with the most popular site in the area being the shore dive at Merimbula Wharf.

The entry and exit at this site is a little tricky, requiring a scramble over the rocks. However, once in the water you have a lovely rocky reef to explore in depths from 3m to 15m. You can also explore under the jetty, which is a good place to see Smooth Stingrays – just watch for fishing lines dangling from above. I actually start my dives by exploring the sand beyond the reef, as this is where the more unusual fishes are seen.

This sandy desert is a great spot to see Smooth Stingray, flatheads, gurnards, soles, stingarees, Port Jackson Shark and, if you are lucky, perhaps an Australian Angel Shark. Another fish that hides in the sand here is the Common Stargazer. This strange-looking species has an upturned mouth and eyes on the top of its head, so it can watch for prey to ambush while completely buried in the sand. Around 20 stargazer species are found in Australia, with the Common Stargazer the most widespread in temperate waters and the largest, growing to 75cm long. Stargazers have venomous spines, and some can even generate electric shocks.

Some very special fishes turn up on the sand at Merimbula Wharf. On one dive I encountered a Broad Cowtail Stingray, a tropical species about 1,000km south of its normal range. My best find was a rare Melbourne Skate. Skates look similar to stingrays, yet are very different, as they don't have tail barbs and they are the only

Common Stargazer (*Kathetostoma laeve*).

Melbourne Skate (*Spiniraja whitleyi*).

members of the ray family that lay eggs. Most skates reside in deep water, although fortunately the Melbourne Skate ventures into shallow temperate water. This is Australia's largest skate species, growing to 2.2m in length.

The rocky reef at Merimbula Wharf plays host to a range of temperate fishes, including Eastern Blue Groper, leatherjackets, wrasses, nannygai, perch, cowfish, boxfish, boarfish and even Weedy Seadragon. A search between the rocks will reveal Green Moray, Banded Wobbegong and Crested Hornshark.

The Crested Hornshark is the rarer smaller cousin of the Port Jackson Shark and only found off New South Wales and southern Queensland. It is mostly seen during winter, when it ventures into shallow water to breed. At this time, they also do something a little nasty – they eat the eggs of their cousins!

Crested Hornshark (*Heterodontus galeatus*).

VICTORIA

Victoria has some of the keenest divers and snorkellers in Australia. Each weekend, no matter how cold the weather or water temperature, these brave souls enter the water to explore rocky reefs, shipwrecks and piers. They do this week in, week out because Victoria has some of the best diving in the country, especially its amazing sponge gardens, that are far more colourful than any coral garden on the Great Barrier Reef. They also keep coming back week after week because Victoria has some incredible fishes; more than 870 species are found in state waters, most of which are endemic, making Victoria a great place to fishwatch.

The coastline off Victoria is part of the Great Southern Reef. This is a recently coined term to raise awareness of this exceptional part of Australia's underwater realm, which is largely unknown to most people. The Great Southern Reef encompasses the temperate rocky reefs of Australia, from southern New South Wales to southern Western Australia. It is the only major expanse of coastline that fronts the Southern Ocean, and it is also home to a superb collection of unique fishes.

The rocky reefs and sheltered bays of Victoria are inhabited by a great variety of fishes. The state doesn't have the fish diversity and variety that is found in Australia's tropical waters, however it makes up for this by having many endemic species that are found nowhere else.

Off Victoria, sharks are only occasionally seen, and mostly small harmless species such as Port Jackson Shark, Draughtboard Catshark and Varied Carpet Shark. Rays are far more abundant, with Smooth Stingray, Southern Fiddler Ray, skates and good variety of stingarees to be seen. Victoria is also the only place where you have a chance of seeing a chimaera in Australia, with the Elephant Fish sometimes seen in Western Port Bay.

Pelagic fish are regularly seen off the state, and most popular dive sites are dominated by reef fishes. Commonly observed are a great variety of leatherjackets, wrasses, cowfish, porcupinefish, morwongs, flatheads, flounders, blue devils, blennies and threefins. However, Victorian waters are also home to many special fishes, such as seahorses, pipefish, seadragons, dragonets, frogfish, gurnards, scorpionfish, stargazers, thornfish and weedfish.

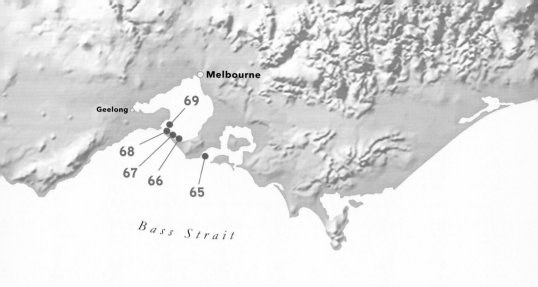

Melbourne, and the magnificent Port Phillip Bay, is the centre of the Victorian dive scene. While offshore are many wonderful rocky reefs and shipwrecks, I have always found the bay and its many delightful piers the best spot for fishwatching. Beyond Melbourne there are many other brilliant diving and snorkelling spots, including Wilsons Promontory, Port Campbell, Warrnambool and Portland. Unfortunately, my diving experience at these destinations is limited, so I haven't included any hot-spots from these areas, even though I am sure there are many.

The water off Victoria may be a little cool, but donning a thicker wetsuit or a drysuit is well worth the effort to see some unique southern fishes.

Located at the entrance to Western Port Bay, Flinders Pier is a wonderful dive site and the best spot in Victoria to see Weedy Seadragon. The pier is very different to the ones found in Port Phillip Bay, as dense beds of seagrass grow all around the jetty and provide a habitat for many fishes.

The average depth under Flinders Pier is only 4m, making it shallow enough for Weedy Seadragons to be observed by both divers and snorkellers. The ones seen off Victoria have very muted colours, not as vibrant as the ones seen off New South Wales and Tasmania. Both adult and juvenile seadragons can be observed, mostly feeding on tiny mysid shrimps.

The pylons of Flinders Pier are decorated with sponges, ascidians and algae, and play host to numerous fishes, including leatherjackets, blennies and weedfish. My favourites are the Thornfish. This is the most common member of the small thornfish family, which have a large spike projecting from their gill cover. This species is mistakenly called a Dragonet, but it is not a member of the dragonet family. Endemic to southern waters, the Thornfish is a pretty fish that likes to sit on pylons, so they are very easy to find and photograph.

Thornfish (*Bovichtus angustifrons*).

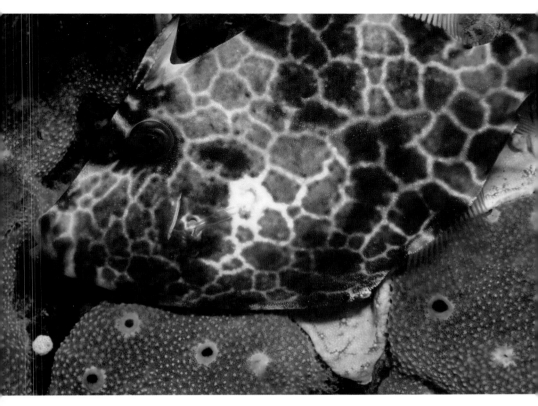

Gunn's Leatherjacket (*Eubalichthys gunnii*).

Several species of leatherjacket are seen here, with the Gunn's Leatherjacket a special one to look for. More common on deeper reefs, these honeycomb-patterned leatherjackets regularly visit Flinders Pier. You generally don't see them swimming across the bottom as they like to hide under the seaweed. This species gets to 60cm in length, however the ones seen here are under 30cm long. The Gunn's Leatherjacket is an endemic species, only found off Victoria, Tasmania and South Australia.

Other reef fishes seen at this site include Rock Flathead, morwongs, Bluespotted Goatfish, wrasses, Old Wife, Globefish and damsels. Smooth Stingray, Melbourne Skate and the occasional stingaree have also been observed under the pier.

The most entertaining fish observed here is the Ornate Cowfish. Cowfish are a type of boxfish with horns on their head and body. These armour-plated fish are slow swimmers, so have a hard external carapace to protect them from predators.

Male Ornate Cowfish (*Aracana ornata*).

The Ornate Cowfish is endemic to southern waters and is a joy to watch as it slowly explores the bottom. The males and females have very different colour patterns, with the males blue and yellow and the females yellow, cream and brown. At most dive sites the females are more commonly seen, however at Flinders Pier both sexes seem to be observed in equal numbers.

66 RYE PIER, RYE

ort Phillip Bay is a huge body of water, covering an area of 2,000 sq km. Numerous piers jut into the bay, with the most popular ones with divers and snorkellers found on the Mornington Peninsula. All these piers are great for fishwatching, although the following three are extra special.

Rye Pier is 300m long, with depths under the pier varying from 2m to 6m. The sea floor under the jetty is mostly sand, with a few rocks and pieces of debris also thrown in. Sponges, seagrass, algae and ascidians sprout from the pylons and bottom, creating food and a habitat for numerous reef fishes.

Typical reef fish seen at Rye Pier include wrasses, weedfish, Moonlighter,

Bigbelly Seahorse (*Hippocampus abdominalis*).

Southern Velvetfish (*Aploactisoma milesii*).

morwongs, Globefish, goatfish, leatherjackets, blennies, Thornfish, flounders, cowfish, Southern Hulafish, gurnards, pufferfish, pike and weed whiting. A few rays are seen here too, mainly Smooth Stingrays and Southern Fiddler Rays.

A very common species seen at Rye Pier is the Bigbelly Seahorse. One of the largest members of the seahorse family, growing to 35cm in length, it is found off the south-east coastline of Australia. These lovely fish vary in colour, and can be cream, yellow, orange or brown, and some even have a mottled pattern. Many also have horn-like filaments on their heads, while others lack this headgear. Bigbelly Seahorses are seen under Rye Pier clinging to seaweed or debris. They are sometimes observed slowly swimming across the bottom, with their tiny fins madly fluttering to drive them forward. The rarer Shorthead Seahorse is also found here, but it likes to hide in the seaweed so is much harder to find.

One of the most interesting fish found at Rye Pier is the Southern Velvetfish. This wide-ranging species occurs throughout the temperate waters of southern

Australia, except for Tasmania. It is common under Rye Pier, and it is possible to find two or three on a single dive if you are prepared to look. The only problem is that they are extremely well camouflaged, and even get algae growing on their skin to conceal their presence. They also don't like to swim much, and prefer to move across the bottom by rocking from side to side like a piece of drifting seaweed. The Southern Velvetfish can grow to 23cm in length and feeds on small crustaceans.

Rye Pier is also a great night dive, and while the crustaceans and molluscs are the main attraction, quite a few fish can also be seen. Night is the best time to find flounders, flatheads and eels, with the occasional Longfinned Worm Eel emerging from the sand to hunt. After dark is the only time to observe Little Gurnard Perch. These small fish grow to 12cm long and hide in the sand by day. At night they scatter across the sand looking for small crustaceans to feed on. Like all gurnards they have venomous spines, and quite a few swimmers have stepped on them accidently.

Little Gurnard Perch (*Maxillicosta scabriceps*).

67 BLAIRGOWRIE PIER, BLAIRGOWRIE

Blairgowrie Pier is part of a large marina complex, so care must be taken to avoid boats. It is also one of the best shore-diving sites in Australia, playing host to an incredible range of invertebrates and fishes.

When I first dived Port Phillip Bay this pier didn't exist, as construction only started in 2001. Considering how little time it has been around, the pylons of this pier are completely encrusted with sponges, algae, seaweed, ascidians and soft corals. The secret of its success is its location on a point, meaning the pier is constantly washed by a gentle cross-current bringing nutrients to feed its abundant marine life.

The sandy bottom under the pier is 2m to 6m deep and the site gets all the typical reef fish seen at Rye Pier, so I will avoid repeating them, but it also attracts more rays and sharks. Commonly seen are Smooth Stingray, Southern Fiddler Ray and Spotted and Sparsely-spotted Stingarees, while the much rarer Thornback Skate turns up from time to time. Banded Wobbegong, Port Jackson Shark and Australian Angel Shark have also been seen at Blairgowrie Pier.

However, it isn't the reef fishes or sharks or rays that make Blairgowrie Pier such a special spot, but all the strange and unusual fishes it attracts. Bigbelly Seahorses

Ringback Pipefish (*Stipecampus cristatus*).

Tasselled Frogfish (*Rhycherus filamentosus*).

are common, and so are pipefish. Widebody, Spotted and Port Phillip Pipefish have been observed on the sand, with the most common pipefish seen here being the Ringback Pipefish. Looking like a stick, these pipefish rarely move, so look for a stick with eyes and a turned-up mouth. Endemic to southern Australia, it is thought

Greenback Flounder (*Rhombosolea tapirina*).

that they migrate into Port Phillip Bay to breed during summer, and this is when I have mostly seen them. The Ringback Pipefish grows to 25cm in length and is best seen in areas of algae and shell debris.

Other strange fish seen at Blairgowrie Pier include Common Stargazers, Sculptured Seamoths and Southern Velvetfish. However, the prize fish is the Tasselled Frogfish. This weird endemic species has the most elaborate camouflage, being covered in growths that look exactly like the algae that grows on the pylons. Even though they grow to 23cm in length, they are not an easy fish to find, and if you want to see one you need to slowly inspect every inch of every pylon. Tasselled Frogfish are very good parents, with the female laying eggs on a solid surface and the male sitting on them until they hatch.

Another bizarre fish seen occasionally at Blairgowrie Pier is the Greenback Flounder. Mostly seen at night, they can get quite large, growing to 45cm in length. They have a strange-looking face, dominated by a large nose that hangs over the mouth. Like other flounders they like to hide under a layer of sand, however I have seen large ones simply resting out in the open.

68 PORTSEA PIER, PORTSEA

Located close to the mouth of Port Phillip Bay, Portsea Pier is very different to Rye Pier and Blairgowrie Pier. The two other sites have powdery silt-like sand, while Portsea has more coarse beach sand and also has more kelp growing under and around the pier. These small variations may seem minor, but this change in habitat means that many different fishes can be seen at this site.

This pier is quite short, only 150m long, and the maximum depth under the pier is 6m. It plays host to more reef fishes than the other piers, with good populations of leatherjackets, wrasses, morwong, Old Wife, Bluespotted Goatfish, Scalyfin, cowfish and Globefish.

It is also one of the best spots to see weedfish. Australia's temperate waters contain around 30 species weedfish and these small fish like to hide in seaweed and algae, so are easily overlooked. Johnston's, Rosy and Wilson's Weedfish have all been

Longnose Weedfish (*Heteroclinus tristis*).

Painted Stinkfish (*Eocallionymus papilio*).

observed at this site, with the most frequently seen member of the family being the Longnose Weedfish, which can grow to 30cm in length, although ones that large are rarely seen. These cryptic fish usually blend in with the seaweed, being either brown or reddish in colour, however some bright yellow ones can also be observed. Weedfish feed on small fish and invertebrates and give birth to live young. After mating, the female retains her eggs internally until they hatch and are expelled. To spot a weedfish, closely inspect the seaweed and kelp.

Sharks and rays are often seen at Portsea Pier. Smooth Stingray and stingarees make regular appearances, and if you swim wide of the pier you may find a rarer Thornback Skate. Draughtboard Catsharks have also been spotted here, even though they generally prefer deeper water.

Seahorses, pipefish and Weedy Seadragon also turn up, while other unusual fish

Goblinfish (*Glyptauchen panduratus*).

to look for include Tasmanian Clingfish, Sculptured Goby and Prickly Frogfish. The sandy shell-rubble bottom is also a good place to look for Painted Stinkfish. This is another delightful member of the dragonet family, unfortunately labelled with a terrible common name, because their skin smells when removed from the water. It grows to 13cm in length and varies in colour from cream to brown. Like other dragonets, they slowly walk across the bottom using their pectoral fins like feet.

Portsea Pier is also the best place to see one of Australia's weirdest fish, the Goblinfish. A member of the scorpionfish family, it is endemic to southern Australia. These strange fish have a square head and big eyes, making them one of the only fish with a discernible neck. They are nocturnal feeders, so spend the day hiding on the bottom, generally under seaweed. Summer appears to be the best time to see Goblinfish at Portsea Pier, as they may enter the bay to breed.

69 POPE'S EYE, PORTSEA

In the 1880s a series of forts were constructed in Port Phillip Bay for the defence of Melbourne. Pope's Eye was meant to be one of these forts, but it was never completed. To create the fort, tons of bluestone rock were dumped on a sand bank, creating a horseshoe-shaped structure, 2m deep at the centre and 12m deep outside. Today Pope's Eye is a marine park, a great dive site and a haven for fishes.

The rocky wall at Pope's Eye is covered in kelp, algae and sponges, and makes a great habitat for reef fishes. This is a very good spot to see many black-and-white striped reef fishes, including Longsnout Boarfish, Old Wife, Magpie Perch, Zebrafish and Moonlighter. Other common reef fishes include Senator Wrasse, Barber Perch, Ornate Cowfish and a good variety of leatherjackets.

Juvenile Scalyfin (*Parma victoriae*).

Globefish (*Diodon nicthemerus*).   Eastern Shovelnose Stingaree (*Trygonoptera imitata*).

A common species here is the Scalyfin. This large member of the damsel family is endemic to southern waters and grows to 25cm long. The adults vary in colour from light brown to black, with the juveniles much prettier being orange with neon-blue spots and lines. For much of the year Scalyfin are easily ignored, except during summer when they breed and become very territorial, attacking other fish and divers who get too close to their nest of eggs. I can tell you I am more fearful of a territorial Scalyfin than any shark, and having been bitten on the head by one, and it drawing blood, I treat them with a high level of respect!

Another species to look out for here is the Globefish. The smallest member of the porcupinefish family, only growing to 30cm in length, it is endemic to Australia's temperate seas. They are quite secretive by day, hiding under kelp or in recesses, and feed on small crustaceans at night. Globefish have toxic flesh to deter predators, and can also swallow water to pump themselves up to look like a spiky globe. I am always happy to encounter a Globefish as they have a permanent smile on their face.

Less common species seen here include Weedy Seadragon, Port Jackson Shark, Smooth Stingray and Shorthead Seahorse. I have also seen an Eastern Shovelnose Stingaree at this site. This is one of the largest members of the stingaree family, growing to almost 1m in length, and it is only found off the south-east corner of Australia, with Port Phillip Bay the best place to see one. Like other stingarees it feeds on small invertebrates it digs from the sand. This species is mostly observed resting on the bottom, sometimes covered in a layer of sand, and other times proudly out in the open.

TASMANIA

Situated in the cold waters of the Southern Ocean, Tasmania is not high on most divers' lists of places to get wet. However, these same nutrient-rich temperate waters feed a wealth of unique and endemic fish species.

Tasmania is a very popular holiday destination, with most visitors exploring the state's topside attractions and rarely venturing below the waves. This is a pity, as the state has some spectacular diving on rocky reefs covered in some of the most beautiful sponge gardens on the planet. Around Tasmania divers can explore rocky reefs, sea caves, shipwrecks and artificial reefs.

The island has a vast coastline and a surprising variety of marine habitats for fishes, including sheltered bays, rocky reefs, sponge gardens, seagrass beds, kelp beds and giant kelp forests, although these have sadly disappeared off the east coast. There are also some interesting estuary habitats, with Hobart's Derwent River home to some very unusual fishes, while on the wild west coast is the unique Port Davey with its tannin-stained waters reducing the light so much that deepwater fishes are seen in the shallows.

Naturally you don't see as many fish species in Tasmania as you do in the tropics, but most of the species you do see are endemic to southern Australia. Around 820 fish species are waiting to be seen in Tasmania, including some interesting sharks and rays, with it the best place to see a Draughtboard Catshark, Banded Stingaree and Thornback Skate. Typical reef fishes include leatherjackets, boarfish, morwongs, wrasses, perch, damsels and a variety of scorpionfish. Schools of pelagic fish are also regularly sighted. One of the features of diving in Tasmania is seeing unusual fishes like seahorses, seadragons, weedfish and gurnards.

Diving services are unfortunately limited in Tasmania, with only a handful of dive shops and charter boats in operation. The west coast and much of the north coast are not accessible unless you have a private boat, and even one of the state's most popular destinations, Bicheno, recently lost its dive operation. Fortunately, there are some great shore-diving sites, although getting hire gear and air fills can be a challenge.

The water temperature off the island is not as cold as many think. The east coast is washed by the East Australian Current, which has unfortunately seen the demise

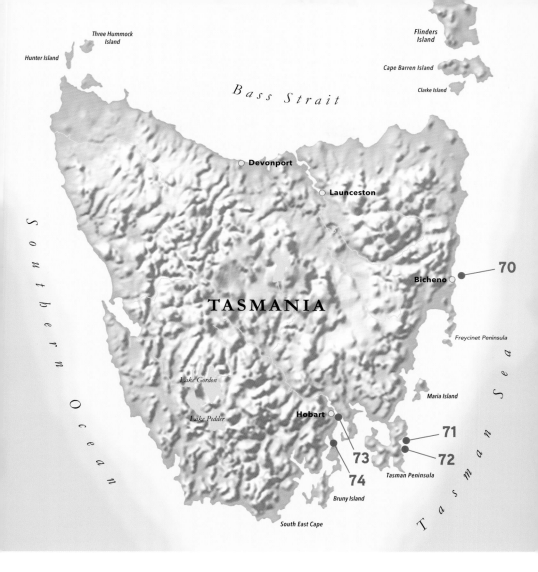

Three Hummock Island

Hunter Island

Flinders Island

Cape Barren Island

Clarke Island

Bass Strait

Devonport

Launceston

Southern

TASMANIA

Bicheno 70

Freycinet Peninsula

Lake Gordon

Maria Island

Ocean

Lake Pedder

Hobart 71

73 72

74 Tasman Peninsula

Tasman Sea

Bruny Island

South East Cape

of the giant kelp forests, but it also means that the water temperature during summer can reach 18°C. This warmer water also brings algal blooms that can sometimes reduce the visibility, while in winter the water temperature drops to 12°C but the visibility can be more than 30m.

Finally, Tasmania is the only place you can see one of Australia's strangest fish families, the handfish, which is a great reason to brave the cold water and head to the Apple Isle.

Bicheno is a small holiday and fishing town on the east coast of Tasmania, roughly halfway between Launceston and Hobart. It boosts the sunniest weather and the warmest climate in the state, and has some of the best beaches. And in the Governor Island Marine Reserve it also has some of Tassie's best diving.

Governor Island creates a natural harbour at Bicheno, and on its eastern side are spectacular rocky reefs covered in beautiful sponge gardens. Divers can see a wonderful variety of fishes at all the dive sites in the area, with Bird Rock a favourite for fishwatching.

The rocky reef around Bird Rock drops to 30m, but most diving is in the 10m to 20m range, where there are caves, gutters and walls to explore. If you start deep, you may see Tasmania's most common ray, the Banded Stingaree. This endemic species is found from southern New South Wales to South Australia, with Tasmania the

Banded Stingaree (*Urolophus cruciatus*).

Southern Conger Eel (*Conger verreauxi*).

only place where they are regularly sighted. They grow to 50cm in length and have a pretty banded pattern across the back. Although small, stingarees have a sharp tail spine for defence, which they generally don't use unless threatened or stepped on. During the day the Banded Stingaree is mostly seen resting on the bottom, sometimes covered in sand and other times out in the open.

Common reef fish seen at this site include Bluethroat Wrasse, Banded Morwong, Shaw's Cowfish, Bastard Trumpeter, Bluespotted Goatfish, Snakeskin Wrasse, Zebrafish and Brownstriped Leatherjacket. This is also a good spot to see schools of Longfin Pike, Silver Trevally and Butterfly Perch.

A common reef fish seen on most rocky reefs around Tasmania is the Longsnout Boarfish. These very distinctive black-and-white fish grow to 50cm in length and often shelter in caves and overhangs. Boarfish are closely related to batfish, and the family contains around 14 species, many of which are only found in deep water. They all have long dorsal fins, and the ones on the Longsnout Boarfish are thought to be venomous. This species is endemic to southern Australia and it makes a great subject for photography.

Longsnout Boarfish (*Pentaceropsis recurvirostris*).

With plenty of ledges and caves at Bird Rock, there are some interesting fishes to be seen. Divers can observe Southern Red Scorpionfish, Marblefish, Largetooth Beardie, Rosy Perch and maybe a Southern Conger Eel. These eels like to hide in caves by day and hunt the reef at night for fish, crustaceans and cephalopods. They can get quite large, growing to 2.2m in length. This eel is found in temperate waters off New South Wales, Victoria, South Australia and Tasmania.

Conger eels are not generally considered dangerous, although a few have bitten divers. In the 1990s there was a very friendly resident Southern Conger Eel at Bird Rock that the Divemasters use to hand feed. Not something that is generally recommended or condoned these days.

71 NOBBIES WALL, EAGLEHAWK NECK

Eaglehawk Neck is the most popular dive destination in Tasmania with a great variety of sites. In the area you can dive deep and shallow rocky reefs covered in kelp and beautiful sponge gardens, explore Tasmania's most famous shipwreck, the *Nord*, investigate sea caves, and even swim with fur seals.

Nobbies Wall is a delightful rocky reef with lots of gutters, ledges and crevices to explore in depths to 25m. Kelp covers much of the rock, and under the kelp are encrusting sponges and colonies of yellow zoanthids. Exploring the reef you will encounter Longsnout Boarfish, Shaw's Cowfish, Marblefish, Banded Morwong, White-ear and a good variety of perch and leatherjackets.

Bluethroat Wrasse (*Notolabrus tetricus*).

Johnston's Weedfish (*Heteroclinus johnstoni*).

A number of endemic wrasses are found on this rocky reef, including Purple Wrasse, Rosy Parrotfish and Senator Wrasse. The most common member of this family you will see is the Bluethroat Wrasse. These large fish can grow to 50cm in length, and while found from Sydney to Adelaide, they are mostly seen off Tasmania. The male is a bluish-orange colour with a distinctive white band, while the smaller female is a greenish-brown colour, and like all wrasses the male has a harem of females. The Bluethroat Wrasse is one of the dominant reef fish of Tasmania, unfortunately their numbers have declined as they are targeted by anglers.

Don't be afraid to look under the kelp at Nobbies Wall, as this green layer shelters a number of interesting fish. You might find Bigbelly Seahorse, Weedy Seadragon, Globefish, Thornfish, Common Gurnard Perch or maybe a weedfish. On one dive here I was very surprised to encounter a Johnston's Weedfish. This is the largest member of the weedfish family, reaching a length of 40cm. Considering how big these fish can get, they are just as cryptic as their cousins and difficult to find. The Johnston's Weedfish is endemic to the south-east corner of Australia.

At Nobbies Wall you are also likely to see Banded Stingarees on the sand or hiding under the kelp. This is also a great spot to see the most common shark species of Tasmania, the Draughtboard Catshark. The catsharks are a large family of sharks, however most species live in deep water and are rarely seen. Of the family, the Draughtboard Catshark is one of the largest, growing to 1.5m in length, and it also prefers shallow water. This species is found from southern Western Australia to southern New South Wales, with Tasmania being one of the best places to see them.

The Draughtboard Catshark has a unique ability to swell its body by ingesting water. This is a defence mechanism to deter predators, and it can also be used to wedge themselves in crevices so a predator, such as a fur seal, cannot extract them. These little sharks lay eggs year-round, which can be seen attached to sponges and kelp, with the young sharks emerging after a one-year incubation period. Draughtboard Catsharks feed on small fish, crustaceans and molluscs at night, and by day they like to hide under the kelp. I have had many wonderful encounters with these small sharks over the years and have found that some are shy and flee from humans, while others are happy to have a diver closely inspect them.

Draughtboard Catshark (*Cephaloscyllium laticeps*).

Eaglehawk Neck is famous for its towering sea cliffs, many of which are riddled with caves. The most impressive cliffs are found at Waterfall Bay, and here divers can explore the largest sea cave in Australia at Cathedral Cave.

This massive cave has three entrances, with the main passage big enough to drive a bus through. Beyond this is a network of smaller tunnels that should only be explored by experienced cave divers. While the cave is fascinating, I like to explore the rocky reef at this site, as it has a good variety of fishes in depths to 25m.

Not many fish are seen inside the cave, except for groups of Bigscale Bullseye. However, a search might reveal a Largetooth Beardie or a Southern Red Scorpionfish. Many years ago the rare Pink Handfish could be seen in Cathedral Cave. Sadly this species, as is the case for most of the handfish, has almost become extinct.

Butterfly Perch (*Caesioperca lepidoptera*).

Male Weedy Seadragon (*Phyllopteryx taeniolatus*) with eggs.

The rocky reef outside of the cave has boulders and ledges to investigate that are covered in sponges, yellow zoanthids and kelp. If you are lucky you may spot a Weedy Seadragon hovering among the kelp. Also called the Common Seadragon, this iconic Aussie fish is found in temperate waters throughout southern Australia and grows to 45cm in length. Their colour patterns, which help to camouflage them against seagrass and kelp, varies from state to state, with the Tasmanian ones having some of the most vivid colours. Male seadragons, like their seahorse cousins, have taken over the main parenting duties, with the male sticking the eggs on their tail until they hatch. Finding Weedy Seadragons is often very difficult as they blend in with the kelp – you just have to watch for a piece of weed that not only moves side to side, but up and down as well.

The rocky reef at Cathedral Cave is also a great spot to see dense schools of Butterfly Perch. These pretty fish are the temperate version of a basslet, and both are members of the groper family. They are mostly observed darting back and forth as they feed on zooplankton. This species also feeds on small benthic invertebrates. It grows to 30cm in length and its range extends from southern Queensland to

Banded Morwong (*Chirodactylus spectabilis*).

southern Western Australia, with Tasmania being one of the best places to see them. When in a dense school they are often joined by other perch species and Sea Sweep.

All the typical Tasmanian reef fishes can be seen on this rocky reef, including the Banded Morwong. This large member of the morwong family can grow to 1m in length, and it is a very important reef fish in Tasmania as it feeds on small sea urchins. One of the reasons that the giant kelp forests have disappeared is because of an increase in sea urchin numbers, due to climate change, resulting in the urchins feasting on the kelp. It is thought that Banded Morwong keep sea urchin numbers in check, so if attempts to regrow the giant kelp are successful, the Banded Morwong could play an important role. Like other morwongs these fish prefer to sit on the bottom, and they tend to be a little more nervous than their northern cousins.

Hobart is not generally a name associated with diving, however there are some very interesting dive sites off Tasmania's capital city. A good variety of reef fish can be seen on the rocky reefs around Bruny and Betsey Islands, if you can organise a dive boat. For some really interesting and unique fishes you need to dive closer to Hobart in either the Derwent River or the D'Entrecasteaux Channel.

A number of shore-diving sites are found in both areas, and divers can explore rocky reefs and sandy bays. A spot close to Hobart where I found some interesting fishes is Bellerive Beach.

This site is quite shallow, with a maximum depth of only 8m, and while there is a great deal of sand to explore, there are also numerous rocky outcrops. These rocky reefs provide food and shelter for a variety reef fishes – look for Southern Hulafish, Senator Wrasse, Variable Threefin, Little Weed Whiting, Globefish and Black Bream. Heading over the sand you are likely to see Longsnout Flounder, Ringed Pufferfish, Southern Bluespotted Flathead and quite a few Southern Sand Flatheads.

Thornback Skate (*Dentiraja lemprieri*).

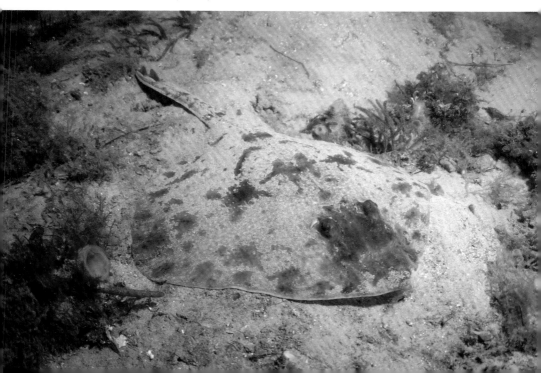

Southern Sand Flathead (*Platycephalus bassensis*).

This vast sandy plain is also a good spot to see Tasmania's most common rays, the Banded Stingaree and the Thornback Skate. Around 50 skate species are found in the seas around Australia, but most live in deep water, so are never seen by snorkellers and divers. The Thornback Skate is one of the few exceptions, entering shallow bays off Tasmania and Victoria. This species grows to 50cm in length and at Bellerive Beach you can often find a few as you explore the sand.

In 1992 I observed some fascinating Thornback Skate behaviour when I watched one walking with its fins. I came across it slowly moving across the bottom, and it wasn't swimming, instead using the tips of its pelvic fins to slowly walk. It was possibly looking for prey, and found this technique allowed it to move with more control. It has since been discovered that several skate species walk this way.

One of my most exciting fishwatching days happened near Bellerive Beach when I saw my first Spotted Handfish. Handfish are relatives of the anglerfish that walk across the bottom on hand-like fins. They also have a head lure, but don't appear to

Spotted Handfish (*Brachionichthys hirsutus*).

use it. These weird fish are only found in southern Australia, and mainly Tasmania, with 14 species in the family.

The Spotted Handfish is only found in the Derwent River area, and studies have found that they rarely move far from where they hatch. They breed in spring, with the female laying a clutch of eggs she attaches to the substrate. She then guards the eggs until they hatch seven to eight weeks later. These small fish grow to 15cm in length and are ambush predators, feeding on small invertebrates.

Sadly, all handfish are under threat from extinction, due to their small range, habitat loss and invasive species such as the North Pacific Seastar eating their eggs. The Spotted Handfish is doing better than most, however it is still critically endangered, as only nine fragmented populations remain. A recovery plan has been put into action for this species and two other handfish, and we can only hope that they save these unique Aussie fishes.

Tinderbox is located at the northern entrance to the D'Entrecasteaux Channel and is one of the most popular shore-diving sites near Hobart. This interesting dive site has a little bit of everything – a rocky reef, seagrass, kelp, algae, sponges and patches of sand, rubble and shell grit. The main reef at Tinderbox is only 3m to 10m, although it is possible to get deeper if you head out into the channel.

This is a good location to see reef fishes. Commonly observed are Sixspine Leatherjacket, Toothbrush Leatherjacket, Bluethroat Wrasse, Banded Morwong, Southern Hulafish, Globefish, Purple Wrasse and a variety of perch. Schools of Silver Sweep, Yelloweye Mullet and Longfin Pike are often seen here.

This is also a good place to see the very cute Shaw's Cowfish. These endearing fish, which have permanently puckering lips, are found throughout the temperate waters of southern Australia and grow to 25cm in length. The males are coloured with a psychedelic pattern of blues and yellows, while the females have a more subdued pattern of browns and creams. They feed on small invertebrates, which they find buried in the sand by blowing, and are always entertaining to watch, making great subjects for photography. Cowfish have spines for defence, however these spines can also cause them problems. While diving at Tinderbox I found a female Shaw's Cowfish that has become wedged upside-down in a crevice due to its spines. She was lucky I came along to release her.

Female Shaw's Cowfish (*Aracana aurita*).

Right: Senator Wrasse (*Pictilabrus laticlavius*).

Below: Southern Red Scorpionfish (*Scorpaena papillosa ergastularum*).

A common reef fish seen darting among the seaweed and kelp at this site is the Senator Wrasse. These pretty fish are found throughout southern waters, and reach a length of 30cm. The males are green with red stripes and blue spots, while the females and juveniles are reddish-brown. They feed on small invertebrates and are thought to live up to ten years. The males can be quite territorial during the breeding season, while the females simply pass through their boundaries without concern.

Weedy Seadragon and the rare Spiny Pipehorse have been seen at Tinderbox, but you are more likely to see their cousin, the Bigbelly Seahorse. Also keep an eye out for Tasmanian Blenny, Common Gurnard Perch and Pencil Weed Whiting. A number of sharks and rays are spotted here, so look for Smooth Stingray, Banded Stingaree, Draughtboard Catshark and Thornback Skate.

Tucked away in the nooks and crannies at Tinderbox are quite a few Southern Red Scorpionfish. I am not sure why they have red in their name, as they come in a variety of colours, and most of the ones I have seen have been yellow, brown or black. This species is the most abundant scorpionfish in Tasmania, although its range extends into New South Wales, Victoria and South Australia. It grows to 30cm in length and like other members of the family it is an ambush predator that feeds on small fish and invertebrates. You generally don't have to look too hard to find one, as they like any rocky outcrop as an ambush spot.

Simpson
Desert

Great Victoria

Desert

SOUTH

AUSTRALIA

Q

Great Australian Bight

Anxious Bay

Eyre
Peninsula

Spencer Gulf

Coffin Bay

Coffin Bay Peninsula

78

Yorke
Peninsula

Gulf St Vincent

Adelaide

Cape Catastrophe

Cape Spencer

79

Kangaroo
Island

77

76

75

Cape Jaffa

SOUTHERN   OCEAN

Discovery Bay

Geelo

King
Island

SOUTH AUSTRALIA

Two fish attract most divers and snorkellers to South Australia – the Leafy Seadragon and the Great White Shark. While the state is the best place to see these two iconic species, there are plenty of other wonderful fishes waiting to be seen.

Washed by the cool temperate waters of the Southern Ocean, South Australia is blessed with some of the most interesting diving in the country. Divers and snorkellers can explore rocky reefs, sponge gardens, shipwrecks, artificial reefs and more than 50 jetties. These provide a habitat for more than 770 fish species, most of which are endemic to these southern waters.

While the Great White Shark is one of the main attractions in South Australia, and can be viewed from the safety of a cage at the Neptune Islands, other sharks and rays are sometimes seen when diving and snorkelling. Port Jackson Shark and wobbegongs are the main sharks seen, while Southern Fiddler Ray, Smooth Stingray and a variety of stingarees are the most common rays. Schools of pelagic fish are encountered at many offshore sites, while an abundance of temperate reef fish are seen on every reef and under every jetty. However, what makes South Australian waters special is their exceptional endemic fishes, such as frogfish, prowfish, weedfish, snake blennies, seahorses and seadragons.

Most of South Australia's underwater attractions are located in the centre of the state, near Adelaide, in the mostly sheltered waters of the Spencer Gulf and the Gulf of St Vincent. Jutting into these gulfs are three long peninsulas – Fleurieu, Yorke and Eyre – that always offer somewhere calm to dive no matter the prevailing seas and winds. South Australia also has many islands that offer great diving, with Kangaroo Island famous for its seals and seadragons. The coastline east and west of this central region is rarely dived, as it is exposed to the roar power of the Southern Ocean. Diving is possible year-round off South Australia, and water temperatures vary from 21°C to 13°C.

A limited number of dive shops and charter boats are located around Adelaide and a few nearby centres. However, much of the state lacks dive facilities. Boat diving is possible at a few locations, however South Australia also has many amazing shore-diving sites, especially its many jetties, and these are some of the best fishwatching sites in the country.

75 PORT NOARLUNGA REEF, ADELAIDE

The coastline off Adelaide has many lovely sandy beaches that are wonderful for beach lovers, and not so great for divers and snorkellers. Fortunately, south of the city, off the town of Noarlunga, is a fabulous rocky reef that can be explored from the shore and is home to a great assortment of fishes.

Port Noarlunga Reef runs parallel to the shore and is accessible via a jetty. The reef is protected as a marine reserve, and divers can explore the inner reef, which is 3m to 9m deep, or the outer reef that drops to more than 20m. The rocky reef on both sides is covered in algae, seaweed, kelp and sponges, and with plenty of ledges and gutters it is a great habitat for a wide variety of fishes.

A very common reef fish seen here is the Magpie Perch. The common name is a bit misleading as this fish is a member of the morwong family. Found throughout Australia's temperate waters, it feeds on benthic invertebrates that it snatches from

Magpie Perch (*Pseudogoniistius nigripes*).

Wavy Grubfish (*Parapercis haackei*).

the sand. Like other morwong, these fish spend most of the day sitting on the bottom, and they are generally easy to approach.

A wealth of reef fish are seen on every dive, including Bluespotted Goatfish, Sea Sweep, Moonlighter, Yellowhead Hulafish, Silver Drummer, Sixspine Leatherjacket, Scalyfin, Zebrafish, Longsnout Boarfish, Rainbow Cale, Old Wife, Ornate Cowfish and Blackspotted Wrasse.

Another common reef fish seen in sandy areas is the Wavy Grubfish. These curious fish feed on small crustaceans and will often follow divers, especially ones who are a little clumsy with their fins and stir up the bottom. It is always fun to interact with curious fishes, and I often attract Wavy Grubfish closer to me by digging in the sand. This species is endemic to South Australia and southern Western Australia and reaches a length of 10cm.

This site also has many ledges that are worth investigating, as these provide homes for Southern Blue Devil, Estuary Catfish, Bigscale Bullseye, Port Jackson Shark and the occasional Cobbler Wobbegong. A few rays can also be seen at Port Noarlunga Reef – look for Western Shovelnose Stingaree, Southern Eagle Ray, Smooth Stingray and Southern Fiddler Ray.

Southern Fiddler Ray (*Trygonorrhina dumerilii*).

The Southern Fiddler Ray is probably the most common ray, either found buried in the sand or resting under the kelp. They grow to 1.4m long and are found from Victoria to southern Western Australia. In this area there are Southern Fiddler Rays that have a unique black-and-white pattern, and for many years they were thought to be a different species. However, recent DNA testing has revealed that they are simply a different colour morph.

The reef is also a good spot for unusual fishes, if you are prepared to look. Divers have seen Crested Pipefish, Port Phillip Pipefish, Western Cleaner Clingfish, Common Weedfish, Goblinfish, Oyster Blenny, Common Stargazer and Painted Stinkfish.

Rapid Bay Jetty is one of the most popular shore dives in South Australia for one main reason – Leafy Seadragon. This site is considered to be the best place to find these iconic Aussie fish, but I have never had much luck finding them here. However, there are plenty of other fishes that make this a great fishwatching spot.

The site is located 100km south of Adelaide. The original jetty was built in 1942 for the loading of limestone from a nearby mine. After the mine closed in 1991 the jetty slowly deteriorated, and was finally closed to the public in 2004. A new jetty was constructed next to the old one in 2009. Both jetties can be dived, with the old one being home to the best fish life.

The old jetty is 470m long with a 200m-long T-section at the end. Depths under the jetty vary from 5m to 9m, and even though the water is shallow it is not possible to explore the entire length of this large jetty in a single dive. Also, if you rush, you will miss many of the unusual fishes.

Reef fish abound, so expect to see a great range of leatherjackets and wrasses, plus Old Wife, Magpie Perch, Moonlighter, Bluespotted Goatfish, Dusky Morwong, Banded Seaperch, Scalyfin, Rough Bullseye, Zebrafish and many others.

Ringed Pufferfish (*Omegophora armilla*).

Western Talma (*Chelmonops curiosus*).

An interesting reef fish seen under the jetty is the Ringed Pufferfish. This species is endemic to southern waters and is easily identified by the black ring around the pectoral fins. It grows to 25cm in length and feeds on small invertebrates found in the sand. Watching them feed is fascinating, as they blow away the sand to uncover potential prey.

One of the prettiest reef fish seen here is the Western Talma. This temperate member of the butterflyfish family is only found off South Australia and southern

Western Australia. Like their tropical cousins, they are often seen in pairs, slowly moving across the reef and picking at the algae looking for worms and crustaceans.

Sharks and rays are occasionally seen at Rapid Bay Jetty, including Southern Fiddler Ray, Western Shovelnose Ray, Southern Eagle Ray and Western Shovelnose Stingaree, or perhaps a Gulf Catshark if you are very lucky. Also keep an eye out for Harlequin Fish, Southern Blue Devil, Silver Trevally, Yellowtail Kingfish and Longsnout Boarfish.

Leafy Seadragons linger around the seaweed under and around the jetty, however, they are not the only unusual fish to be seen. A keen eye may also spot Southern Velvetfish, Tasselled Frogfish, Prickly Frogfish, Goblinfish, Rhino Pipefish or Brushtail Pipefish.

A cute little fish found here, mainly at night, is the Tasmanian Clingfish. These tiny fish hide under rocks and debris during the day, and emerge at night to feed. The species is endemic to southern waters, and while they have Tasmania in the name, they are mostly seen off South Australia. These lovely little fish grow to 8cm in length, and are observed clinging to the fallen pylons under the jetty.

Tasmanian Clingfish (*Aspasmogaster tasmaniensis*).

77 EDITHBURGH JETTY, EDITHBURGH

Edithburgh is a small coastal town on the Yorke Peninsula. It has an interesting history that centres around its jetty, which was built to load ships with local produce. Today the old jetty is a hot-spot for diving, and each weekend dozens of divers descend on the town to explore one of the best dive sites in Australia.

The first Edithburgh Jetty was constructed in 1873 for the loading of cargo, and since then it has been rebuilt many times. The current jetty is 170m long and is mainly used by anglers. Fortunately for divers, access steps give easy entry and exit in and out of the water.

Depths under Edithburgh Jetty vary from 2m to 7m, and divers and snorkellers can explore a forest of pylons covered in a colourful coating of sponges, ascidians and tubeworms. Seagrasses grow all around the jetty, while the sandy bottom and accumulated debris below the jetty have plenty of hiding spots for a wonderful variety of fishes.

Numerous reef fish are seen on every dive, including Ornate Cowfish, Zebrafish, Western Talma, Moonlighter, Magpie Perch, Bluespotted Goatfish, Wavy Grubfish, Rough Bullseye, Yellowtail Scad, Sea Sweep, Globefish and a good variety of wrasses and leatherjackets. Sharks and rays are less common, however you might be lucky and see a Western Shovelnose Stingaree, Port Jackson Shark, Banded Wobbegong, Southern Eagle Ray or Coffin Ray.

Many small fish are found at Edithburgh Jetty. Some of the easier ones to locate are Crested Threefin, Thornfish, Painted Stinkfish, Sculptured Goby and Tasmanian Blenny. You may also be fortunate to find a Leafy Seadragon feeding in the seaweed.

Dusky Snake Blenny (*Ophiclinus antarcticus*).

Prickly Frogfish (*Echinophryne crassispina*).

A prize find for me was a small Prickly Frogfish hiding among the debris on the bottom. This endemic frogfish is found from southern New South Wales to South Australia and only grows to 7cm long. It is a very cryptic fish, and spends most of its time hidden from view, often under rocks and old oyster shells. They feed on tiny decapod crustaceans and breed in early summer. This is not the only frogfish species that is found here, as divers have also seen Whitespotted, Tasselled and the bizarre Narungga or Naked-rod Frogfish, which looks like an ascidian.

At night you are likely to find a few Tasmanian Clingfish. I also spotted a rarer endemic, the Southern Sole. Little is known about this secretive little fish, which buries itself in the sand by day and emerges at night to feed. Some soles have toxins they can secrete from a gland for defence, but there is no information about the Southern Sole having toxins.

Edithburgh Jetty can also lay claim to having the best collection of unusual endemic fish seen anywhere in Australia. The only problem is finding them, as like the frogfish most are cryptic, camouflaged or very well hidden. Some of those unusual fishes include Shorthead Seahorse, Spotted Pipefish, Longsnout Pipefish, Widebody Pipefish, Sculptured Seamoth, Longfinned Worm Eel, Spadenose Clingfish and Warty Prowfish.

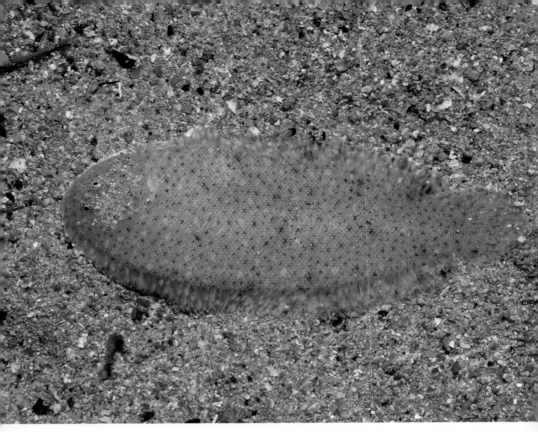

Southern Sole (*Aseraggodes haackeanus*).

I was very lucky to find a Dusky Snake Blenny on one dive. Snake blennies are in the same family as the weedfish, although they have a more elongated body. The Dusky Snake Blenny is only found off South Australia and southern Western Australia, and likes to hide under rocks and debris. I was looking for frogfish when I found this one under a broken clump of sponge. Little is known about this species, and it is thought to feed on amphipods.

Another brilliant South Australian jetty dive located on the western side of the Yorke Peninsula is Port Hughes Jetty. Unfortunately, this site can be a washout when strong westerly winds are blowing, especially during the cooler months. When it can be dived, Port Hughes Jetty is home to a wonderful array of fishes.

This jetty is around 250m long, with depths varying from 3m to 7m. Like all South Australian jetties, the pylons are encrusted with sponges, soft corals, ascidians and kelp, while the sea floor under the jetty is a mix of sand, seaweed, debris and old pylons. All these habitats provide a great home for a wonderful variety of reef fishes.

This is a great spot to see Shaw's and Ornate Cowfish. These cute boxfish are hard to miss as they slowly swim between the pylons. Other common reef fishes include Tasmanian Blenny, Little Weed Whiting, Blue Weed Whiting, Ringed Pufferfish, Wavy Grubfish, Magpie Perch, Western Talma, Bluespotted Goatfish and Globefish. This is also a good spot to see leatherjackets, with Bridled, Southern Pygmy, Mosaic and Rough Leatherjackets all common.

Between the pylons, divers will also see schools of Sea Sweep, Yellowtail Scad, Rough Bullseye, Wood's Siphonfish and Yellowhead Hulafish. Several sharks and

Gulf Pipefish (*Stigmatopora narinosa*).

Shorthead Seahorse (*Hippocampus breviceps*).

rays can also be spotted, so keep an eye out for Smooth Stingray, Port Jackson Shark, Southern Eagle Ray and maybe a Cobbler Wobbegong.

The best thing about Port Hughes Jetty is the high number of weird and wonderful fishes that can be seen. This is a good spot to see Sailfin Goby, Painted Stinkfish, Southern Velvetfish and Blackthroat Threefin. A special feature of this site are pipefish. In the seaweed divers have encountered Gulf, Spotted, Brushtail, Longsnout and Smooth Pipefish. Of these the Gulf Pipefish is the species most

Whitespotted Frogfish (*Phyllophryne scortea*).

likely to be seen. This pipefish is only found in a limited area of South Australia, and grows to 15cm in length.

While looking for pipefish diver are also likely to find a few Shorthead Seahorses hiding in the seaweed. This small seahorse grows to 10cm in length and is very cryptic, clinging to similarly coloured seaweed and algae. This species is endemic to southern waters, being found off Victoria, South Australia and parts of Tasmania. It is a social seahorse, often found in mixed-sex groups.

Port Hughes Jetty is also a spot to look for frogfish. Tasselled Frogfish have been spotted resting on the pylons, while Whitespotted Frogfish have been observed on the sea floor hiding between old shells. The latter is another endemic frogfish only found in Australia's temperate waters. It grows to 10cm in length and varies in colour to suit its habitat and background. The female lays her eggs on rocks, then her male partner guards them by wrapping his body around the eggs.

79 NORTH NEPTUNE ISLAND, PORT LINCOLN

The remote Neptune Islands lie 60km south of Port Lincoln. Home to seabirds and thousands of fur seals, this isolated island group is surrounded by rocky reefs and would be a fabulous place to dive, apart from one minor detail. The archipelago is home to Australia's largest population of Great White Sharks.

The islands are split into two groups, called North and South, and surrounded by deep water they are visited by many pelagic fish species. With an abundance of fish and seals, the islands are the perfect habitat for these iconic sharks, with researchers identifying more than 1,000 individuals visiting the islands.

For more than 30 years charter boats have been visiting the Neptune Islands and dropping cages into the water so people can view Great White Sharks. This is the only place in Australia where you can see them. These islands are so special that they were declared a marine park in 2012. These majestic sharks are seen at both island groups, but I have picked North Neptune Island as the best place to fishwatch.

Great White Sharks have been demonised in horror films and documentaries as mindless killing machines. However, once you see them underwater you quickly realise they are similar to all sharks – wary of humans, boats and other things they are not too sure about. They have to be lured close by burley and chum, otherwise they would avoid most boats completely. The occasional shark is curious of the humans in the cage, but unfortunately most show no interest and only bump into the cage by accident when chasing baits.

Great White Shark (*Carcharodon carcharias*).

Horseshoe Leatherjacket (*Meuschenia hippocrepis*) and Silver Trevally (*Pseudocaranx georgianus*).

These magnificent sharks grow to 6.5m long, but most seen at North Neptune Island are between 3m and 4m long. Larger females, more than 5m long, are best seen in late autumn and winter. Great Whites are seen here year-round, however they have been known to disappear for weeks or months at a time. A lack of Great Whites often coincides with the arrival of Orca, which are known to prey on the sharks.

Great Whites are not the only sharks seen at North Neptune Island, as Shortfin Mako and Bronze Whaler Sharks are sometimes spotted during summer. If you can jump into an ocean-floor cage you also have a chance of seeing Port Jackson Shark, Varied Carpetshark, Smooth Stingray and Southern Eagle Ray.

Several fish species are also attracted by the burley, including Yellowtail Kingfish, Sea Sweep, Zebrafish and schools of Silver Trevally. The Silver Trevally is only found in the temperate waters of Australia and New Zealand and grows to 94cm in length. At most dive sites it is nice to be surrounded by schools of Silver Trevally, unfortunately they are a little annoying at North Neptune Island as they often swarm around the cage and block your view of the sharks!

Often seen swimming among the Silver Trevally are very bold Horseshoe Leatherjackets. These endemic fish are only seen in southern waters and can reach 60cm in length. They get their strange name for the horseshoe-shaped pattern on their side. This species eats small invertebrates, and is more than happy to nibble on free chum from the charter boats.

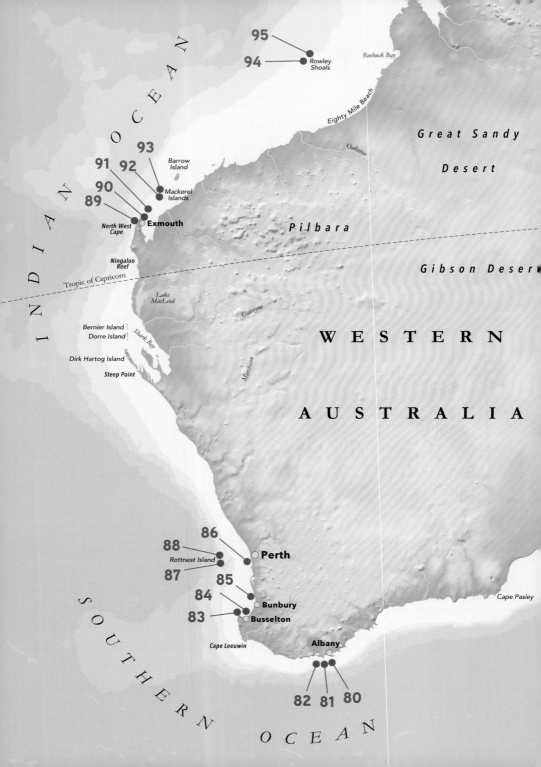

INDIAN OCEAN

95
94 — Rowley Shoals

Roebuck Bay

Eighty Mile Beach

Oakover

Great Sandy

Desert

93
91 92 — Barrow Island
90 — Mackerel Islands
89
North West Cape — Exmouth

Pilbara

Gibson Desert

Ningaloo Reef

Tropic of Capricorn

Lake MacLeod

Gascoyne

WESTERN

Bernier Island
Dorre Island

Shark Bay

Murchison

Dirk Hartog Island

Steep Point

AUSTRALIA

86
88
87 — Rottnest Island — Perth

85
84 — Bunbury
83 — Busselton

Cape Pasley

Cape Leeuwin

Albany

82 81 80

SOUTHERN OCEAN

WESTERN AUSTRALIA

The long and varied coastline of Western Australia stretches from the cool waters of the Southern Ocean to the warm waters of the Indian Ocean. The largest state in Australia has the longest coastline, the most islands, its own fringing coral reef and the greatest variety of marine habitats. And with countless wonderful dive sites it is the perfect place to fishwatch.

Off Western Australia divers can explore coral reefs in the north, limestone reefs in the subtropical and temperate regions around Perth, and brilliant rocky reefs decorated with sponges off its southern temperate coast. Not only this, off the state are isolated atoll reefs at the Rowley Shoals, and the state is also the gateway to the spectacular Indian Ocean Territories of Christmas Island and Cocos (Keeling) Islands.

Western Australia has the only western coastline in the Southern Hemisphere with a warm south-flowing current. Known as the Leeuwin Current, this flow of warm tropical water sweeps down the west coast and wraps into the Great Australian Bight. The Leeuwin Current not only raises the water temperature off Western Australia, but carries corals and tropical fishes into the temperate zone and allows them to flourish.

With such a huge variety of habitats spread across seas from tropical to temperate zones it is no surprise that Western Australia is home to more than 3,290 species of fishes in both saltwater and freshwater. Across the state you can see a wonderful variety of sharks and rays, with the state home to many endemic species of wobbegongs, catsharks, stingrays, stingarees and even numbfish. Western Australia is also the only state where you can reliably see Whale Sharks at the annual migration at Ningaloo Reef. Pelagic fishes are also commonly seen throughout the state.

Reef fishes are abundant off Western Australia, and while many of the tropical species are shared with the east coast, there are also a host of Indian Ocean tropical species that are exclusive to the state. Most of Western Australia's temperate fishes are endemic, with some ranging throughout the temperate zone and others unique to the west. Many endemic fish in this region have west or western in their common name – a good indication that they are unique to Western Australia. A host

of unusual reef fish are also found off the state, including a variety of velvetfish, dragonets, pipefish, frogfish, scorpionfish and seadragons, while it even has its own endemic seahorse.

The diving is fabulous throughout Western Australia, with dive shops and charter boats in most of the major towns. Shore diving and good snorkelling spots are found off the southern and central coasts, although many of Western Australia's best dive sites are only accessible by boat. Liveaboard boats offer trips to the state's island groups and atolls. While you can dive year-round off Western Australia, this vast coastline does have better seasons, with the southern temperate sites best during summer, and the northern tropical sites best in winter. Autumn and spring are generally a good time to explore anywhere in the state.

I have been fortunate to make many trips to Western Australia to explore its exciting dive sites and see a plethora of astonishing fishes. With a state this big, and with most of its coastline still unexplored, it would take a lifetime to see all of Western Australia's brilliant fishes.

Albany was once a whaling town until this barbaric practice was banned in 1978. Today it is a great spot to watch whales, while the old whaling station is now a museum. Divers can also explore one of the old whale-chase boats.

The 47m long *Cheynes III* was scuttled in 23m of water off the western end of Michaelmas Island in 1982. The artificial reef makes for a wonderful dive and is covered in lovely sponges and soft corals. Swimming around the wreckage, expect to see Redband Wrasse, Southern Maori Wrasse, Silver Drummer, Spinytail Leatherjacket, Sea Sweep, Zebrafish and groups of Blackhead Puller. Inside the wreck shelter schools of Bigscale Bullseye, Western Talma, Moonlighter and Southern Blue Devil.

As much fun as the wreck is to explore, the rocky reef around Michaelmas Island is home to a much wider variety of fishes. It is covered in kelp and sponges, and it holds fond memories for me as it was where I saw my first Leafy Seadragon. Found

Leafy Seadragon (*Phycodurus eques*).

from South Australia to southern Western Australia, this is one of the most iconic and highly sought-after fishes in Australian waters. They grow to 35cm in length and have such an elaborate covering of weedy growths that they can be very difficult to find. They hover among kelp and seagrass, feeding on tiny mysid shrimps, and may appear to be slow swimmers, yet a study tracked one moving 150m in one hour. An experienced local guide is always recommended in order to find Leafy Seadragons, and photographers are asked to treat these special fish with respect, so limit photos to avoid stressing the animal.

Exploring this rocky reef you will also encounter Old Wife, Bluespotted Goatfish, Globefish, morwongs, leatherjackets, wrasses and Western Red Scorpionfish. I was lucky to find a rarely seen Bicolor Scalyfin at this site. A search between the boulders might also reveal a Western Jumping Blenny or Blackthroat Threefin.

One unique fish to keep an eye out for is the multicoloured Harlequin Fish. This temperate member of the rockcod family is only found off South Australia and

Harlequin Fish (*Othos dentex*).

southern Western Australia and can reach 80cm in length. Harlequin Fish come in a rainbow of colours, a mix of orange, red, pink and brown, and are covered in either yellow or blue spots. They are long lived, more than 40 years, and unlike other rockcods, the sexes are separate and can't change. Look for Harlequin Fish in caves and under ledges – they generally sit on the bottom, being ambush predators, so are easy to approach.

Sharks and rays can also be found at Michaelmas Island. The occasional Port Jackson Shark, Smooth Stingray or Banded Wobbegong is seen, with the most common elasmobranch being the Striped Stingaree. This endemic little ray is only found around the south-west corner of Western Australia, and is the most common stingaree divers encounter. They grow to 60cm in length and are mostly seen resting between boulders at Michaelmas Island. Little is known about their biology, however like other stingarees they give birth to live young that are miniature versions of the parents.

Striped Stingaree (*Trygonoptera ovalis*).

Another ex-navy ship can be dived off Albany – the former guided missile destroyer HMAS *Perth*. The 133m-long ship is the sister ship of HMAS *Brisbane*, and was scuttled in King George Sound in 2001. The ship now rests at a depth of 35m and is a haven for fishes.

In its time sitting on the bottom the ship has been transformed into a wonderful artificial reef, with the structure covered in sponges, soft corals, ascidians, black corals, anemones and hard corals. Numerous invertebrate species thrive on the ship, attracting a great variety of fishes.

On the outside of the ship divers will see dense schools of Yellowtail Scad. Feeding on these fish are pelagic visitors such as Silver Trevally, Yellowtail Kingfish and Samsonfish. Numerous reef fishes parade around the wreck, including Foxfish, Old Wife, Spinytail Leatherjacket, Blue Morwong, Western Talma and Bluehead Puller. A few Western Blue Gropers can also be spotted. This species is larger than its eastern cousin, reaching 1.7m in length, although I have found them to be far shier.

A less shy wrasse relative seen on the ship in large numbers is the Redband Wrasse. Groups dart among the sponges and ship structure, and if you look closely

Breaksea Cod (*Epinephelides armatus*).

Redband Wrasse (*Pseudolabrus biserialis*).

you will see that this is a male with his harem of females. The males are a darker red colour, while the females have a row of black spots along their upper back. This endemic species is only found off southern Western Australia and South Australia, and grows to 25cm in length. Redband Wrasse feed on small invertebrates they find hiding on this colourful artificial reef.

Another endemic reef fish often seen on HMAS *Perth* is the Breaksea Cod. This member of the rockcod family is only found off southern Western Australia, and reaches a length of 56cm. Like other rockcods they are ambush predators, feeding

Yellowhead Hulafish (*Trachinops noarlungae*).

on small fish they can grab. They vary in colour from black to pink, and because they are popular with anglers they are best seen on sites like this that are marine reserves.

Venture inside the wreck and there are countless rooms and passageways to explore. Residing inside the wreck are Bigscale Bullseye, Harlequin Fish, Globefish, Western Red Scorpionfish and Banded Wobbegong. A number of Southern Blue Devils hide throughout the ship, although more abundant are the Yellowhead Hulafish. Both species, along with the scissortails, belong to the longfin family, however, a future review may split this group. The Yellowhead Hulafish lives in groups and feeds on small crustaceans and fish. Endemic to South Australia and southern Western Australia, it is a difficult fish to study and photograph as it rarely stops moving.

Before surfacing from a dive on HMAS *Perth*, check out the ends of handrails while doing a safety stop, as these provide a home for False Tasmanian Blennies. These cute little fish look very similar to the more widespread Tasmanian Blenny, yet are smaller, 8cm long, and only found off Western Australia.

While there are many wonderful rocky reefs around the shoreline and islands off Albany, one of the area's most unusual dive sites is a legacy of its whaling days. In the bay opposite the whaling station is a site used for dumping whale bones. So many whale bones litter the sandy bottom that they have formed an artificial reef that is now covered in sponges, plate corals and a host of temperate fishes.

The site is called Boneyard, although you are hard pressed to see any whale bones because of the coral coverage. This strange reef varies in depth from 15m to 20m, and the first thing you will notice is vast schools of fish. Schools of Swallowtail Nannygai, Silver Sweep, Western Pomfred and Bigscale Bullseye cover the reef. Darting between them are Zebrafish, Old Wife and Tarwhine.

A very common fish seen at Boneyard is the Moonlighter. This pretty black-and-white fish is closely related to butterflyfish, and is a member of the stripey and mado family, which is only found in Australia and New Zealand. The Moonlighter is the most wide-ranging member of the family, found from southern Western Australia to Victoria. These fish grow to 40cm in length and are often seen in pairs, feeding on

Moonlighter (*Tilodon sexfasciatus*).

Southern Blue Devil (*Paraplesiops meleagris*).

plankton and small invertebrates, while the juveniles have been observed cleaning other fishes.

Boneyard is also a great spot to see Southern Blue Devils, many of which sit on the plate corals. Nearly always found propped up on the bottom on their long pectoral fins, the Southern Blue Devil is one of the most iconic fishes in southern waters. Covered in a polka-dot pattern, these endemic fish are found on rocky reefs from Victoria to southern Western Australia. They grow to 35cm in length, live for up to 60 years, feed on small invertebrates and fish, and are often seen in breeding pairs. They are a great fish to study and photograph, as most are happy to sit still. However, their blue dots can play havoc with the focus system of some underwater cameras.

Other reef fish seen at Boneyard include Foxfish, Brownspotted Wrasse, False Senator Wrasse, Bluespotted Goatfish, Western Crested Morwong, Blue Morwong, Globefish, Western Talma, Horseshoe Leatherjacket and Sergeant Baker. Also check the sand around the reef as you may spot Sparsely-spotted Stingaree, Longhead Flathead, Rock Flathead and maybe a Brushtail Pipefish.

A more thorough search between the corals at Boneyard will also reveal Western Red Scorpionfish, Ringed Pufferfish, Western Jumping Blenny and maybe a Gulf Gurnard Perch. This last fish is a member of the scorpionfish family and endemic to South Australia and southern Western Australia. It reaches a length of 40cm and like other gurnard perch it has large eyes that come in handy for feeding at night on invertebrates and small fish. This species is rarely seen, so have a good look among the plate corals at Boneyard if you want to find one.

Gulf Gurnard Perch (*Neosebastes bougainvillii*).

83 HMAS *SWAN*, BUSSELTON

Busselton is a lovely holiday town located at the southern end of Geographic Bay. The bay is washed by the warm waters of the Leeuwin Current, and as such it has rich coral and sponge gardens and even a few tropical visitors. Off the town, divers and snorkellers can explore numerous rocky reefs, with the big attraction for fishwatchers being an old warship and an old jetty.

That old warship is HMAS *Swan*, a 113m-long River Class Destroyer Escort that was scuttled in 1996. The ship is located off Dunsborough, resting at a depth of 31m, with most visiting dive boats departing from Busselton. The ship is decorated with a wonderful array of sponges and corals, and it takes many dives to properly explore all it has to offer.

Descending onto the ship, the big surprise is the groups of Longfin Batfish that hover around the vessel, as this is a species normally associated with much warmer waters. These fish mix with groups of Old Wife, Globefish, Moonlighter and Yellowtail Scad. Pelagic fish constantly patrol the ship, with Samsonfish, Silver Trevally, Yellowtail Kingfish and Greater Amberjack seen. Under the stern

Dusky Morwong (*Dactylophora nigricans*).

are usually schools of Tarwhine, Sea Sweep, Longfin Pike and Mulloway.

Another fish found in schools around HMAS *Swan* is the Footballer Sweep. This species may have sweep in its name, yet it is another member of the stripey and mado family. These colourful fish are only found off South Australia and southern Western Australia, and grow to 23cm in length. The species obtained its strange name as it was thought that their striking pattern resembled a footballer's jersey. These cute little fish feed on small invertebrates and zooplankton, and are a great subject for photos.

Abundant reef fish gather on the ship, including McCulloch's Scalyfin, Whitebarred Boxfish, Western King Wrasse, Brownspotted Wrasse, Redband Wrasse, Western Blue Groper and a good variety of leatherjackets and morwong.

A shy reef fish occasionally observed is the Dusky Morwong. The largest member of the morwong family, growing to 1.2m in length, this species is very different from other morwong, having an elongated body. They like to sit on the bottom, and are a shy species that will flee when a diver gets close. They feed on benthic invertebrates and are endemic to southern Australia.

A number of unusual reef fishes can turn up here. Keep a lookout for Australian

West Australian Dhufish (*Glaucosoma hebraicum*).

Footballer Sweep (*Neatypus obliquus*).

Pineapplefish, Shaw's Cowfish, Baldchin Groper, Ringed Pufferfish, Longsnout Boarfish and Yellowspotted Boarfish.

Sheltering inside the ship are Southern Blue Devil, Rough Bullseye, Harlequin Fish and West Australian Dhufish. A member of the Pearlperch family, the dhufish grows to 1.2m long and is heavily targeted by anglers. Endemic to Western Australia, it is generally found in deeper water, only entering shallow water to breed during the warmer months. It is a difficult species to photograph as the scales are highly reflective.

Adominant feature of Geographic Bay is the very long Busselton Jetty. First built in 1865, and repaired and extended many times, the current jetty is 1,841m long, making it the longest timber jetty in the Southern Hemisphere. The structure is so long that a train service is used to reach the end, where an underwater observatory is located. While you can simply watch the fish from the observatory, diving or snorkelling Busselton Jetty is highly recommended as it is one of the best fishwatching spots in the country.

The jetty can be dived from the shore, from a platform near the underwater observatory, or from a boat. Whichever way, you will have a great time exploring this wonderland of colourful pylons. The maximum depth under the jetty is 9m, which allows for plenty of bottom time to look for some of the amazing fish that gather at the site.

Under the jetty expect to see dense schools of Rough Bullseye and Yellowtail Scad swarming between the pylons. They are joined by a great menagerie of reef fishes, including Whitebarred Boxfish, Globefish, Western Crested Morwong, Dusky Morwong, Old Wife, Moonlighter, Shaw's Cowfish, Western Talma,

Banded Seaperch (*Hypoplectrodes nigroruber*).

Scalyfin, West Australian Dhufish, Bluespotted Goatfish, Ringed Pufferfish and an incredible variety of leatherjackets and wrasses.

One of my favourite reef fish at Busselton Jetty is the Banded Seaperch. This wide-ranging species is found throughout southern Australia, although it appears to be most common off Western Australia. It likes to sit on the bottom and watch the world go by, grabbing any small fish that comes too close.

Several sharks and rays are seen here from time to time. Smooth Stingray, Masked Stingaree, Southern Eagle Ray, Coffin Ray, Port Jackson Shark and Cobbler Wobbegong have all been spotted. However, the most common elasmobranch found here is the Blackspotted Catshark. This little shark only grows to 67cm in length and is endemic to Western Australia. They are not easy to find (believe me

Rainbow Cale (*Heteroscarus acroptilus*).

Longfinned Worm Eel (*Scolecenchelys breviceps*).

I have looked and not found one yet) as this is a nocturnal species that hides by day.

The seagrass beds around Busselton Jetty also abound with fishes. Hiding here are Pencil Weed Whiting, Senator Wrasse, Longhead Flathead, Silver Pufferfish and many other species. This is a great spot to spy a Rainbow Cale. The cales and weed whitings are only found off Australia and New Zealand, and most typically hide in seaweed. The Rainbow Cale is one of the prettiest members of the family and is found throughout the southern waters of Australia. They reach a length of 24cm, and are a very secretive fish, so finding one is a real treat.

The jetty is also a great spot to see weird and unusual fishes. Divers have seen Giant Frogfish, Glauert's Frogfish, Goblinfish, Western Cleaner Clingfish, Southern Velvetfish, Red Indian Fish, Sailfin Goby and Tasselled Leatherjacket. My prize find was a rare Longfinned Worm Eel. Worm eels are a type of snake eel that burrow in the sand. They feed at night on invertebrates, so I was very surprised when I saw one sliding through the seagrass during the day. This species grows to 60cm in length and is found throughout the temperate waters of Australia.

85 LENA, BUNBURY

A maze of limestone reefs litters the coast off Bunbury, Western Australia's second-largest city. These reefs offer fabulous diving in depths from 8m to 36m. However, most divers travel to Bunbury to dive a pirate ship, the *Lena*.

This 55m-long fishing vessel was discovered fishing illegally in Australian waters, so was captured, stripped and scuttled off Bunbury in 2003. The ship now rests at a depth of 18m and has been transformed from a plunderer of fishes into a haven for fishes.

Swarming around this vessel are schools of Globefish, Longfin Batfish, Longfin Pike, Footballer Sweep and Old Wife. A smaller fish found on the ship in compact schools is the pretty Blackhead Puller. These attractive fish are members of the damsel family, and are endemic to the south-west corner of Western Australia. Only reaching a length of 6cm, they flit about the ship, keeping to their own patch of the

Sharpnose Weed Whiting (*Siphonognathus caninis*).

wreck. When they breed, they pair up and the female attaches her eggs to the ship. The male then fertilises the eggs and guards these precious capsules until they hatch.

Numerous reef and pelagic fish can be seen on the *Lena*. Expect to observe Western Talma, Baldchin Groper, Shaw's Cowfish, Foxfish, Western King Wrasse, Banded Sweep, Moonlighter, Dusky Morwong, Harlequin Fish, Silver Trevally, Samsonfish, Sergeant Baker, Blackspotted Wrasse and Yellowstriped Leatherjacket. Inside the ship, divers can also encounter Southern Blue Devil, West Australian Dhufish, Banded Wobbegong and schools of Rough Bullseye.

The sand, seaweed and rocky reef around the ship is also worth exploring, as more reef fish are found here, including some unusual species. Look for Masked and Sparsely Spotted Stingarees, Longhead Flathead, Snakeskin Wrasse, Rainbow Cale and Banded Sea Perch.

The seagrass is also populated with a strange elongated fish, the Sharpnose Weed Whiting. These endemic fish are found from southern Western Australia to

Blackhead Puller (*Chromis klunzingeri*).

Glauert's Frogfish (*Allenichthys glauerti*).

Victoria, and hiding in dense seaweed they are rarely seen. They grow to 10cm in length, and vary greatly in colour, with the females and juveniles typically brown, red or green, and the males yellow or green with blue spots and lines. Weed whiting are in the same family as the cales, and are closely related to the wrasses. And similar to wrasses, the females can change sex if they lose their male partner.

On the rocky reef near the *Lena* I also found a very strange-looking fish, a Glauert's Frogfish. Looking more like a sponge than a fish, it took me almost a minute to confirm it was actually a frogfish, and that was only established once I located the eye and the head lure. The Glauert's Frogfish is found off South Australia and southern Western Australia, and very few have been seen. This bizarre fish grows to 19cm long and can change its colour to perfectly match surrounding sponges. Like all frogfish it is an ambush predator that flicks a head lure to attract prey.

Northand south of Perth are numerous brilliant shore- and boat-diving sites. In this area divers can explore limestone reefs, shipwrecks, artificial reefs and a number of fascinating jetties. One of my favourite jetties for fishwatching is the Ammo Jetty near Freemantle.

Originally built in 1903, and used for the loading of explosives, the jetty is now only used for recreational purposes, and is popular with anglers, snorkellers and divers. Depths under the jetty reach 9m, and the pylons are completely covered in sponges, soft corals and ascidians.

Hiding in this colourful growth is a very special fish, the West Australian

West Australian Seahorse (*Hippocampus subelongatus*).

Weeping Pufferfish (*Torquigener pleurogramma*).

Seahorse. Endemic to southern Western Australia, these beautiful fish can vary in colour, being white, yellow, pink, grey, brown and even purple. Reaching a length of 25cm, these seahorses also have a striped tiger-like pattern to aid camouflage. For the untrained eye it can be hard to spot a West Australian Seahorse clinging to a similarly coloured coral, but you just need to take your time and look very closely for a horse-shaped head. If you are lucky, you might even see a courtship display, which can last for days, before the female deposits her eggs in the male's pouch.

The Ammo Jetty is a great spot to find a wide variety of reef fish. Commonly seen are Shaw's Cowfish, Western Smooth Boxfish, Fanbelly Leatherjacket, Western Crested Morwong, Western Talma, Stripey, Southern Pygmy Leatherjacket, Bluespotted Goatfish, Globefish, Old Wife, Western Striped Cardinalfish and Wavy Grubfish. Port Jackson Sharks are also found under the jetty, including cute juveniles during summer. Other elasmobranchs seen here include Smooth Stingray, Coffin Ray, Western Shovelnose Ray and Western Shovelnose Stingaree.

Fallen pylons and other debris litter the bottom, providing habitat for many interesting fishes. Estuary Catfish, Striped Catfish, Western Gobbleguts, Blackthroat Threefin, False Tasmanian Blenny and Highfin Moray are usually found. The

Western Dragonet (*Callionymus goodladi*).

endemic Woodward's Moray is also occasionally seen – this rare eel is only found in a small area off southern Western Australia.

The sand around the Ammo Jetty is also a great spot to see unusual fishes. Bearded Velvetfish, Bighead Gurnard Perch, Midget Flathead, Spotfin Tongue Sole and even Black-finned Snake Eel have been sighted.

Hick's, Rusty-spotted and Ringed Pufferfish may also be found, with the most common member from this family being the Weeping Pufferfish. Commonly called a toadfish by most Australians, this member of the pufferfish family is very wide-ranging in temperate waters, from southern Queensland to central Western Australia. The Weeping Pufferfish only grows to 21cm in length and is a feisty little fish, having a go at spearfishers and annoying anglers. They feed on a variety of small invertebrates, and are often found resting half-buried in the sand.

The dragonet family is also well represented at the Ammo Jetty, with Finger Dragonet, Painted Stinkfish and Western Dragonet all common. This last species is only found off Western Australia and grows to 22cm long. Dozens of them are seen either resting on or half-buried in the sand, or slowly moving over the sand sucking up food particles.

87 SHARK CAVE, ROTTNEST ISLAND

Perth divers are very spoilt, as they have brilliant diving along the coast and 18km offshore is the fabulous Rottnest Island. This low-lying limestone island is surrounded by wonderful rocky reefs that are riddled with a network of caves. One of the most popular caves is located off the south-west end of the island and is called the Shark Cave.

The main cave is under a giant slab of rock, and is a great spot to observe Grey Nurse Sharks. Up to a dozen can be observed in the cave or patrolling the nearby gutters, and if you stay still on the bottom, they will closely inspect you. This cave is also loaded with schools of Footballer Sweep, Rough Bullseye, Sea Sweep and Western Pomfred.

Around the main cave the rocky reef is cut by smaller caves, ledges and gutters which are covered in sponges and kelp in depths between 12m and 25m. Exploring this reef, divers will encounter Smooth Stingray, Port Jackson Shark, Striped

Southern Eagle Ray (*Myliobatis tenuicaudatus*).

Male Western King Wrasse (*Coris auricularis*).

Stingaree and maybe a Banded Wobbegong or Southern Eagle Ray. This eagle ray is found throughout the temperate waters of southern Australia; unlike its relatives that are seen soaring through the water column. This species is often observed resting on the bottom, even buried under a layer of sand. These rays reach a width of 1.6m and feed on molluscs, worms and crustaceans. I have noticed that when a Southern Eagle Ray is resting on a rocky reef you can often approach very closely, but if they are swimming around the reef they are quite shy and wary.

The rocky reef around the Shark Cave abounds with reef fish. Commonly seen are Scribbled and Redband Wrasses, West Australian Dhufish, Whitebarred Boxfish, Western Talma, McCulloch's Scalyfin, Old Wife, Moonlighter, Harlequin Fish, Zebrafish, Bluelined Leatherjacket and Foxfish.

One of the prettiest reef fish seen here is the Western King Wrasse, which is another species endemic to Western Australia. These lovely fish are always seen in groups, with a dominant male and his harem of females. This species grows to 40cm in length and feeds on small invertebrates. They are a very flighty fish, especially the larger males, so getting close for photos can be difficult.

Redlip Morwong (*Goniistius rubrolabiatus*).

A number of tropical species are also seen at this site. Divers have seen parrotfish, butterflyfish, angelfish and damsels. One of the most colourful species seen at the Shark Cave is a local speciality, the Redlip Morwong. These dazzling fish are endemic to Western Australia and grow to 40cm long. They are usually seen resting on a ledge, sometimes in caves, and they can be difficult to approach and photograph. Like other species of this family, the Redlip Morwong feeds on small invertebrates, often grabbing mouthfuls of sand to find a meal.

The Slot is a giant cavern located off the north-west end of Rottnest Island. When you first approach there is no indication of how large it is, as the many entrances are small and hidden among the kelp. Upon entering you find yourself in a multi-chambered cavern that is lined with colourful sponges, gorgonians and ascidians.

This main chamber is 18m deep, and home to schools of Rough Bullseye, Western Pomfred and Sea Sweep. Banded Wobbegongs are sometimes found here, as are Western Wobbegongs. Nine of the ten Australian wobbegong species are found off Western Australia, including several species, like the Western Wobbegong, that are endemic to the state. Unfortunately, unlike on the east coast where wobbegongs are common and seen in large numbers, the ones in Western Australia are shy and cryptic, making most of them very difficult to find. I did see a Western Wobbegong

Foxfish (*Bodianus frenchii*).

at The Slot, but it was tucked up in a narrow crevice and almost impossible to photograph.

A species that is much easier to see here is the lovely Whitebarred Boxfish. These armour-plated fish are endemic to southern waters, found from Victoria to southern Western Australia. With its small fins it is a slow swimmer, so often makes a getaway by hiding under ledges. These pretty fish grow to 33cm in length and feed on small invertebrates, especially crustaceans.

The Slot and its surrounding reef are home to a good variety of reef fishes. Divers will observe Southern Blue Devil, Horseshoe Leatherjacket, Western Talma, Old Wife, Harlequin Fish, Western Sea Carp, Redlip Morwong, Western King Wrasse, Southern Maori Wrasse, Yellowstripe Leatherjacket and Baldchin Groper.

Another common reef fish is the Foxfish, which is a member of the wrasse family that reaches a length of 40cm. They are found off both the east and west coasts, yet strangely not in Victoria, so there is a possibility that the two populations are different species. These fish are very photogenic, with their red or orange colouration, and have been known to follow divers hoping for a free feed. Foxfish are long lived, reaching 60 years of age, and are a popular species with anglers.

A few unusual fish to look for at The Slot include Western Cleaner Clingfish,

Largetooth Beardie (*Lotella rhacina*).

Whitebarred Boxfish (*Anoplocapros lenticularis*).

Adelaide Weedfish, Spotty Seaperch and Bluelined Hulafish. In the darker recesses also keep an eye out for Largetooth Beardie. These nocturnal fish grow to 66cm in length and spend the day hidden away in caves. At night they hunt the reef, feeding on fish, crustaceans and cephalopods, which they locate with the aid of chin barbels. The Largetooth Beardie is found throughout the temperate waters of Australia, and is typically a shy and secretive fish. Most observations of this species are brief, as once spotted by torchlight they quickly retreat into a darker hideout.

89 BLIZZARD RIDGE, NINGALOO REEF

Ningaloo Reef is the most famous dive destination off Western Australia. The fringing reef is 260km long and protected as a marine park, and accessible from either Coral Bay or Exmouth. Many wonderful dive sites are found along the reef, with one of the best fishwatching spots located on the inner side of the reef at Lighthouse Bay – a great spot called Blizzard Ridge.

The main feature here is a limestone ridge, 1m to 2m high, that is undercut with ledges in depths from 12m to 14m. The site doesn't have a lot of pretty corals, instead it is overloaded with fishes, including schools of baitfish that can cover the reef like a blizzard.

Panda Butterflyfish (*Chaetodon adiergastos*).

Undulated Moray (*Gymnothorax undulatus*).

This is a great spot for sharks and rays, with Tasselled Wobbegong, Whitetip Reef Shark, Blotched Fantail Stingray and Bluespotted Feathertail Ray all common. Less common elasmobranchs include Leopard Shark, Tawny Nurse Shark, Spotted Eagle Ray, Porcupine Ray and Jenkins' Whipray.

This site is also a great spot for larger fish, with Goldspotted Groper, Blackspotted Groper, Queensland Groper and Potato Cod all resident. Also expect to see a variety of batfish, sweetlips, coral trout, tuskfish, trevally, barracuda and emperors. The list of reef fishes seen at Blizzard Ridge is endless, with many varieties of angelfish, butterflyfish, wrasses, surgeonfish, rockcods, hawkfish, parrotfish, damsels, coral snappers, boxfish, pufferfish, gobies, blennies and scorpionfish, many of which are only found in the Indian Ocean.

One of those fish is the lovely Panda Butterflyfish. Nearly always seen in pairs, they like to slowly weave across the reef looking for coral polyps to eat, especially soft coral polyps. This species is only found off the west coast of Australia and north to the Philippines. Like all butterflyfish they are fabulous photography subjects with their pretty patterns. The trick to getting close to observe and photograph butterflyfish is to take your time and wait for the fish to get comfortable with your

Striped Catfish (*Plotosus lineatus*).

presence. Once this happens, they will start to feed and let you get quite close.

Numerous moray species are found residing in the many nooks and crannies. Look for Giant, White-eyed, Stout and Yellow-margin Morays. The most abundant moray is the Undulated Moray. This wide-ranging species is more common off the west coast than the east, growing to 1.5m long and roaming the reef at night to feed on fish, crabs and octopus.

Blizzard Ridge is also a good spot for unusual fishes. Divers have seen Banded Toadfish, Striped Clingfish, Paleblotched Pipefish, Marbled Snake Eel, Horrid Stonefish, Cockatoo Waspfish and a variety of frogfish and ghostpipefish.

Two catfish species are also seen under the ledges – the endemic Sailfin Catfish and the more abundant Striped Catfish. The latter grows to 35cm and is always found in schools that can number in the hundreds, feeding on small invertebrates they find in the sand. Watching a group feeding is very entertaining, as they move quickly across the bottom and constantly leapfrog each other to get to the front. These catfish have venomous spines, so show them some respect and don't get too close. Although a tropical species, it has been seen as far south as Perth and Sydney.

In the 1960s the US military built a pier at Point Murat, near Exmouth, to supply their top-secret base, the Harold Holt Naval Communication Station. For decades the pier was off-limits, then in the 1990s divers were invited to explore the site, and what they found was extraordinary – one of the greatest collections of fishes on the planet. Today the Navy Pier is one of the world's best spots for fishwatching.

Located in the Exmouth Gulf, the pier is tidal, so best dived on the high tide. It is 150m long with a T-section at the end. Depths under the pier vary from 10m to 15m, and beside the colourful pylons, divers can explore sand and a limestone reef.

Swarming around the pylons are immense schools of coral snappers, trevally, fusiliers, batfish, bannerfish, emperors and sweetlips, while resting on the crossbeams are Blackspotted and Goldspotted Gropers. On the bottom divers will encounter Whitetip Reef Shark, Tasselled Wobbegong, stingrays, morays, coral trout, tuskfish

Giant Frogfish (*Antennarius commerson*).

Banded Toadfish (*Halophryne diemensis*).

and more gropers. Joining this mass of fish is an endless parade of reef fishes too numerous to mention.

As wonderful as all these fish are, it is the unusual fish that make the Navy Pier such a special dive site. A search of the sand and rocky reef will reveal shrimp gobies, pipefish, catfish, blennies, glider gobies, dragonets, soles, flatheads, ghostpipefish and maybe a rare Northern Wobbegong.

The pier is also a great spot to see frogfish, with Giant Frogfish the species most commonly encountered. The largest member of the family, growing to 45cm in length, it has the longest lifespan too at around five years, whereas most small frogfish only live for a year or two. Found in tropical and subtropical waters throughout the Indo-Pacific region, Giant Frogfish are generally seen alone, only getting together to breed. And after this happens the male doesn't outstay his welcome, for fear of being eaten by the female!

A search of the many ledges and recesses may also reveal a Banded Toadfish. This

Goatee Velvetfish (*Pseudopataecus carnatobarbatus*).

species is found throughout Australia's tropical waters, with the best place to see one being the Navy Pier. This toadfish reaches a length of 28cm and can vary in colour from cream to brown. It is an ambush predator and feeds on a variety of food items that can be grabbed – everything from small fish to sea stars. These fish are great photography subjects, as they smile at you from their lair. Just don't get too close as they have sharp spines that can inflict a painful wound.

When I first dived the Navy Pier in 2006, I found a very unusual fish that I had never seen before. It was a multicoloured velvetfish, which was later described in 2012 and given the common name of Goatee Velvetfish. This well-camouflaged fish is only found off the north-west coast of Western Australia, most often at the Navy Pier. Little is known about this velvetfish, except that it grows to 10cm and is an ambush predator. It is seeing unusual fish like this that makes the Navy Pier such a top fishwatching spot.

91 FRAGGLE ROCK, MURION ISLANDS

North and South Murion Island are located north of Ningaloo Reef, and are visited on day trips from Exmouth. These islands are ringed by limestone reefs that offer wonderful snorkelling and diving, with Fraggle Rock a superb place to fishwatch.

Considering how close the Murion Islands are to Ningaloo Reef, the diving here is very different. At Fraggle Rock the rocky reef varies in depth from 9m to 15m, and divers can explore gutters, ledges, caves and one large bommie. Soft corals, hard corals, sponges, gorgonians and ascidians decorate this colourful reef.

Numerous reef fish are seen here, including Blue Angelfish, Greencheek Parrotfish, Goldspotted Sweetlips, Blackspot Snapper, Coral Rockcod and a good variety of wrasses, surgeonfish, damsels, hawkfish, goatfish and butterflyfish.

A lovely reef fish seen at Fraggle Rock is the Forceps Butterflyfish. These pretty

Leopard Blenny (*Exallias brevis*).

Lunartail Bigeye (*Priacanthus hamrur*).

fish are nearly always seen in pairs, and they are quite territorial, chasing away other Forceps Butterflyfish from their patch of reef. They feed on coral polyps, fish eggs, hydroids, small crustaceans and even the tentacles of echinoderms, all of which is snatched via their long beak.

Swimming around Fraggle Rock you are also likely to encounter Blotched Fantail Stingray, Bluespotted Feathertail Ray, morays, gropers and Tasselled Wobbegong sheltering in the caves. Other fish seen in caves at this site include Scribbled Pufferfish, Barred Soapfish, Red Squirrelfish and groups of Ringtail Cardinalfish.

These caves are also home to a few Lunartail Bigeyes, which are nocturnal fish with rather large eyes to help them see in the dark. They spend the day hidden in caves or under ledges, emerging at night to feed on small fish and invertebrates. This tropical species grows to 40cm. Although generally a red colour, it can quickly change to silver or a blotched pattern. They are mostly seen alone, although they sometimes form into schools and roam the reef by day.

Fraggle Rock is also a good spot to see the endemic Australian Anemonefish. This fish is only found in the north-west of Australia. Other small reef fish seen here

Forceps Butterflyfish (*Forcipiger flavissimus*).

include gobies, threefins and blennies, including the cute Leopard Blenny. These gorgeous little fish live in the branches of hard corals and feed on coral polyps. Leopard Blennies are very photogenic, but getting one to sit still for a photo is never easy. They often lead photographers on a merry chase, appearing on a different branch of the coral every few seconds.

The Mackerel Islands are located off the town of Onslow, and are not a destination that many people have dived or snorkelled. I was fortunate to go there when a dive operation was in business and was astonished by the wonderful diving and the abundance of fishes.

There are dozens of great dive sites around the largest island in the group, Thevenard Island, and we even discovered a few new spots on exploratory dives. One shallow site I loved for its great fish life was Rob's Bommie.

Located off the south-west end of Thevenard Island, this site is only 3m to 6m deep, and dotted with a series of coral heads. Many of these are riddled with crevices, which are occupied by the rare Northern Wobbegong. One of the smallest members of the wobbegong family, growing to 63cm in length, this species is only found off the northern coast of Western Australia. It has a more subdued pattern than its

Northern Wobbegong (*Orectolobus wardi*).

relatives, and is just as lazy, spending most of the day resting under ledges. Not a great deal is known about this secretive little shark, and even its range is still unclear.

At Rob's Bommie I spotted a large Tawny Nurse Shark squeezed under a ledge. It was so tightly wedged that its hitchhiking Slender Suckerfish was getting squashed. A member of the remora family, the suckerfish is the most common member of this family that spend their lives clinging to sharks and other large marine animals. Eight species of remoras are found around the world, with the Slender Suckerfish found in tropical to warm temperate waters. This species grows to 1.1m long and, like other remoras, clings to its host with a modified dorsal fin that acts like a suction cap. Remoras may look like a large parasite, getting a free ride and stealing their host's food, yet they do provide some cleaning services. However, they do annoy their hosts, which are sometimes observed rubbing against the bottom to dislodge these freeloaders.

The ledges at this spot also provide a home to morays, lionfish, cardinalfish and soapfish, while swimming between the coral heads are a good variety of parrotfish, sweetlips, wrasses, angelfish, damsels, butterflyfish, coral snappers and Blacktip Reef Shark.

Slender Suckerfish (*Echeneis naucrates*) clinging to a Tawny Nurse Shark.

Striped Threefin (*Helcogramma striatum*).

A number of small fish are also seen at Rob's Bommie. Have a look for juvenile Yellow Boxfish, Palespotted Combtooth Blenny and Piano Fangblenny. I spotted a lovely Striped Threefin sitting on a gorgonian. These small fish only grow to 4cm in length and spend most of their day on a perch watching for passing zooplankton they can eat. Although found in tropical waters across the north of Australia, the Striped Threefin is mostly seen off Western Australia.

93 BLACK FLAG, MACKEREL ISLANDS

When first dived this site was marked by a black flag as a good fishing spot, so it got stuck with this strange name. However, it was easy to see why an angler marked the spot as it is overloaded with fish. The rocky reef here varies in depth from 9m to 17m, and is riddled with gutters, ledges, caves and walls, creating shelter for a variety of fishes.

As soon as you enter the water at Black Flag you are surrounded by fishes. Schools of Round Batfish, Fiveline Snapper, Stripey Snapper, Grey Drummer, Golden Trevally and Smallmouth Scad swarm across the reef. The most impressive schooling fish are the Threadfin Pearl Perch. This species is found in tropical waters across northern Australia, although they are generally only seen off Western Australia. Four species of pearl perches are found in Australia, and all have big eyes as they mostly inhabit deep water. The Threadfin Pearl Perch grows to 32cm in length and has long filaments trailing from its fins. Always found in schools, these fish feed at night on crustaceans and cuttlefish.

Among the schooling fish at Black Flag divers will also see Red Emperor

Threadfin Pearl Perch (*Glaucosoma magnificum*).

Scribbled Pufferfish (*Arothron mappa*).

Snapper, Ribbon Sweetlips, Goldspotted Sweetlips, Spotted Coral Trout, Yellow Boxfish, Blue Angelfish, Scribbled Angelfish and Baldchin Groper. Smaller reef fish include an assortment of damsels, butterflyfish, goatfish, surgeonfish, wrasses, scorpionfish and rockcods. Keep an eye out for pelagic visitors such as Grey Reef Shark, mackerel, barracuda and queenfish.

Gropers are common at Black Flag, while another large resident to look for is Scribbled Pufferfish. The patterns on this species vary considerably, from a covering of wavy lines to spots or a mixture of both. Found in tropical waters throughout the Indo-Pacific, this species grows to 65cm in length and feeds on sponges, algae and small invertebrates. Scribbled Pufferfish have quite an elaborate mating ritual that starts with the male excavating a nest in the sand. Within the nest he creates geometric patterns, and when a female visits he swims above the nest to show off his work. If she is impressed she will lay her eggs for him to fertilise.

Northern Rock Flathead (*Cymbacephalus parilis*).

The many caves and ledges at this site are filled with bullseyes, squirrelfish, soldierfish and cardinalfish. These ledges also provide a resting spot for Bluespotted Feathertail Stingray, Tawny Nurse Shark, Tasselled Wobbegong, Whitetip Reef Shark, Giant Moray, Common Lionfish and Zebra Lionfish.

The sandy bottom at Black Flag is also home to some interesting fishes, including shrimp gobies, Gracile Saury, Mural Glider Goby and Northern Rock Flathead. This last species is one of the prettiest members of the flathead family, covered in a mosaic pattern that aids with camouflage. The Northern Rock Flathead is an ambush predator that feeds on small fish and crustaceans. This species grows to 51cm in length and is found in tropical waters throughout Australia, yet it is another species mostly seen off Western Australia.

94 CLERKE WALL, CLERKE REEF, ROWLEY SHOALS

T here are not many places you can dive and snorkel along the northern coast of Western Australia, as the inshore waters are murky and home to Saltwater Crocodiles. However, 300km off the coast of Broome are three wonderful coral atolls known as the Rowley Shoals.

These remote reefs can only be visited on a liveaboard vessel, for a few weeks in spring, meaning only a limited number of visitors enjoy this special location each year. All of the reefs have incredible diving, and with more than 650 species of fish they are a great spot to fishwatch.

Clerke Reef is at the centre of the Rowley Shoals and has a large sheltered lagoon, plus coral walls and healthy coral gardens to explore. Clerke Wall is located at the southern end of the reef and drops from the surface to more than 50m.

Patrolling this wall are Grey Reef Shark, Giant Maori Wrasse, Rainbow Runner,

Meyer's Butterflyfish (*Chaetodon meyeri*).

trevally, barracuda, mackerel, tuna and Wahoo. If you are lucky you might also see a Silvertip Shark or Sailfish.

Schools of Bumphead Parrotfish are best found in the morning, while Steephead, Spotted and Whitespot Parrotfish can be seen at any time. Other large reef fish seen at Clerke Wall are Potato Cod, Bluespotted Coral Trout, Camouflage Groper and a variety of sweetlips, surgeonfish and coral snappers.

Numerous angelfish and butterflyfish are seen, including the pretty Meyer's Butterflyfish. These lovely fish are always seen in pairs as they slowly roam the reef looking for food, which appears to be coral mucus. The Meyer's Butterflyfish is a wide-ranging tropical species of the Indo-Pacific, yet I have mainly seen them on deeper oceanic reefs. Like all butterflyfish they are pelagic spawners, releasing their eggs and sperm into the water column to drift with the currents to other reefs. This species grows to 18cm in length and is best approached when preoccupied with feeding.

Other common reef fish include a great variety of damsels, wrasses, triggerfish,

Blue Fusilier (*Caesio teres*).

Allen's Combtooth Blenny (*Ecsenius alleni*).

rabbitfish, hawkfish, basslets, goatfish, pufferfish and rockcods. Large schools of Blue Fusiliers constantly sweep up and down the wall. Like all fusiliers, these fish feed on zooplankton, snapping them up as they patrol the reef. The Blue Fusilier grows to 40cm long and is a common tropical species in northern Australia.

A close inspection of the corals that decorate Clerke Wall will reveal many small fishes like Old Glory Goby, Eyelash Fangblenny, Redfin Threefin and Yellow Coralgoby. A close investigation of the gorgonians might also reveal a few Denise's Pygmy Seahorses. My close inspection of the corals revealed a few endemic Allen's Combtooth Blennies. These tiny fish grow to 4cm in length and are only found on the offshore reefs of northern Western Australia. They are named after the famous ichthyologist Gerald Allen, who first discovered the species. Allen's Combtooth Blennies eat algae, and are mostly seen sitting on the bottom and keeping an eye out for passing predators.

95 BLUE LAGOON, CLERKE REEF, ROWLEY SHOALS

The coral gardens and coral canyons at Blue Lagoon are one of the most popular dive sites at Clerke Reef. This site varies in depth from 12m to 25m, and has some stunning corals and a good variety of fishes.

As you explore this site you will find numerous ledges and caves. These provide shelter for bullseyes, soldierfish, squirrelfish, soapfish, cardinalfish, lionfish and quite a few Whitetip Reef Sharks.

The Whitetip Reef Shark is a member of the large whaler shark family, which look and act very differently to their close relatives. They have a short broad snout, a long thin body, and are often found sleeping in caves during the day. Most of their close relatives have to keep swimming in order to pump water though their gills, while this species is able to suck in water through its mouth while stationary. They are very active at night, stalking the reef to feed on fish, octopus, cuttlefish and crustaceans. To find their prey they squirm under ledges and into coral crevices.

Female Whitetip Reef Shark (*Triaenodon obesus*) with mating scars.

Doublebar Goatfish (*Parupeneus crassilabris*).

I found many Whitetip Reef Sharks resting in the caves at Blue Lagoon, and also spotted one very active female. While trying to photograph her I realised why she was so nervous, as she had very fresh mating scars (bite marks near her gills) so was probably trying to avoid males while she healed.

Grey Reef Sharks are common at Blue Lagoon, and the area might be a nursery for this species, as we saw several juveniles that were less than a metre long. Also keep an eye out for Reef Manta Rays as they glide through the area.

At Blue Lagoon divers will encounter schools of Bluestriped Coral Snapper, barracuda, parrotfish, fusiliers and trevally. Other large fish at the site include Potato Cod, Dogtooth Tuna and numerous Bluespotted Coral Trout.

An abundance of reef fish dart around the coral gardens, including Ornate Butterflyfish, Teardrop Butterflyfish, Lei Triggerfish, Purple Queenfish, Golden Damsel, Peacock Rockcod, Emperor Angelfish, Oriental Wrasse and many others.

One fish often seen zigzagging across the reef is the Doublebar Goatfish. Goatfish are overlooked by many divers and snorkellers, yet they are interesting to

Checkerboard Wrasse (*Halichoeres hortulanus*).

watch as they feed. They have two long barbels that protrude from the chin, which they use to dig through the sand for prey. These barbels have chemo-sensors that help the fish to locate worms, crustaceans and other invertebrates. This goatfish is a wide-ranging tropical species, and mostly seen on offshore reefs. It grows to 38cm in length, and like other goatfish can quickly change colour. Some goatfish use this colour-changing ability to mimic the colours of schooling fish, so they blend into the crowd.

Another attractive fish seen at Blue Lagoon is the Checkerboard Wrasse. Like all wrasse this species has different colour patterns for juveniles, females and males. They are often observed following other fish around, and rudely snatching any food the other fish uncovers. Checkerboard Wrasse eat a variety of invertebrate species and grow to 27cm long. Found in the tropical north of Australia, it is not an easy fish to photograph as it never stops moving.

Make sure you check the sandy bottom beyond the coral gardens as many small fishes reside here, as does a large colony of Spotted Garden Eels.

96 FLYING FISH COVE, CHRISTMAS ISLAND

Most Australian's associate Christmas Island with illegal boat people. However, this island paradise should be better known for its abundant wildlife, seen above and below the water line. Located south of Java, Christmas Island is really part of Asia, but this external Australian Territory is one of the best places to fishwatch in Australia.

This large island is the peak of a basalt sea mount, that rises 5km off the surrounding sea floor. As such there are sheer walls covered in coral right around the island, and a surprising number of sea caves to explore. The dive operators on the island have more than 40 dive sites to explore by boat, but the most popular dive site is accessible from the shore – the amazing Flying Fish Cove.

Simply walking off the beach, or jumping off the end of the jetty, gives divers and snorkellers access to the pretty coral gardens that flourish in this cove. The coral reef

Ornate Hawkfish (*Paracirrhites hemistictus*).

Tyler's Toby (*Canthigaster tyleri*).

slopes gently to the edge of the drop-off, and then plummets to 400m. However, most diving is done in depths above 20m. While the corals are nice, the best thing about this dive site is the vast number of fish species that are easily observable, including many that are rarely or never seen around the Australian mainland.

The wonderful fish life starts in the shallows under the jetty, where a large school of Fivebar Flagtails swarm between the pylons and greet every visitor. Feeding between the rocks and pylons are Orangeblotch Surgeonfish and a good variety of wrasse species, including quite a few Rockmover Wrasse. Also under the jetty look for False Stonefish, numerous goatfish, parrotfish, grubfish and quite a few Lined Soapfish. However, the fish that I keep an eye out for are the Wedgetail and Blackpatch Triggerfish. Both species are a little shy of divers, but with a little patience you can get quite close to observe and photograph them.

At the coral gardens the fish life gets even better. Here divers will see many familiar reef fishes, and many species that are unique to this part of the Indian Ocean. Populating this zone is a wide variety of butterflyfish, angelfish, surgeonfish, scorpionfish, rock cods, hawkfish, fusiliers, basslets, wrasses, parrotfish and pufferfish.

Sitting on every available outcrop are Ornate Hawkfish, a species rarely seen elsewhere in Australia. They are quite a large hawkfish, growing to 29cm long, and most boldly hold their position as you closely inspect them. Other unique fishes seen in these coral gardens include Powderblue Tang, Meyer's Butterflyfish, Gilded Triggerfish, Foursaddle Groper and Guineafowl Puffer.

Moving to the drop-off, first look out into the blue as pelagic fish, Spotted Eagle Rays and even the occasional Whale Shark might make an appearance. Turn left at the drop-off and divers will come across a large patch of knobbly coral that is infested with moray eels. The species most commonly seen is Masked Moray, but also look for Giant and Yellowmargin Morays. A few years ago a spectacular Dragon Moray could be seen in this area, but unfortunately it has moved on.

Other unique fish to look for on this drop-off include Tyler's Toby, Blue-eye Damsel and groups of Yellowback Anthias. Two very special endemic angelfish can also be seen in this area, the Cocopeel and the Cocos Pygmy Angelfish. Both species are small and easily overlooked, and contribute to making this a very special fishwatching site.

Cocos Pygmy Angelfish (*Centropyge joculator*).

97 FLYING FISH COVE BY NIGHT

Flying Fish Cove has so many unique fish species that it deserves two spots in the top 100. Being an easy shore dive, this site is also an excellent night dive where a whole different set of unique fishes can be seen.

Like most night dives, this site plays host to a great range of crustaceans and echinoderms that emerge to feed after sunset. Divers are also likely to see a few squid and octopus under the jetty.

Entering from the shore, the first active fish species you are likely to see is the Stocky Hawkfish. This species is found across the Indo-Pacific region, yet I had never seen one until I dived Flying Fish Cove at night. Seeing several darting about I suddenly realised why I had never seen this species before – because it is nocturnal. All other hawkfish feed by day, while the Stocky Hawkfish feeds after dark on crabs and other small invertebrates.

Tiger Snakemoray (*Scuticaria tigrina*).

Stocky Hawkfish (*Cirrhitus pinnulatus*).

Among the rocks under the jetty also look for sleeping fish. Butterflyfish, damsels and wrasses tuck themselves away here to stay safe from predators. Nighttime predators on the prowl include Flowery Flounder and Smooth Flutemouth.

More sleeping fish are found on the nearby coral gardens, and some more active squirrelfish, cardinalfish, pufferfish and a good variety of lionfish. Common, Dwarf and Spotfin Lionfish are abundant, so watch where you place your hands as a jab from one of these fish is a very painful experience. The rarest of all the lionfish can also be seen here, the secretive Twinspot Lionfish. This species is much shier than its cousins and will disappear into a hiding spot if you show it too much attention.

Morays are also seen in the coral gardens. Snowflake and Yellowmargin Morays are the most common species, seen with their heads poking out of a lair. Often a resident Giant Moray, more than 2m long, can also be encountered. Several rarer moray species can be seen by torchlight, and we were lucky enough to see a Yellow-headed Moray snaking across the bottom looking for a meal.

A completely unexpected moray also turned up on one of our night dives at Flying Fish Cove – a Tiger Snakemoray. Snakemorays are a less common family of

Crocodile Snake Eel (*Brachysomophis crocodilinus*).

morays that lack the long dorsal and anal fins of true morays, which makes them appear more snake-like. This slow-moving eel was exploring every nook and cranny on a coral head, and allowed us a few minutes to observe it before it disappeared into a dark hole.

The sandy bottom between the coral gardens might look dull and devoid of marine life, yet this zone is full of surprises. Little flatheads, lizardfish and soles can be seen here, and one of our group also found a small pipefish. However, sharp eyes are needed to see the most unique fishes here – snake eels. Both Crocodile and Marbled Snake Eels reside in the sand, and with only their small heads exposed they are not easy to find.

98 PERPENDICULAR WALL, CHRISTMAS ISLAND

There are countless walls for divers to explore at Christmas Island, and washed by currents most are decorated with beautiful corals. Of all the wonderful walls around this large island the pick of the bunch is Perpendicular Wall.

This dive starts in a large overhang cave lined with beautiful gorgonians, and then divers drift along a vertical wall that is cut by numerous ledges and smaller caves. The corals that drape this wall are simply exquisite – a patchwork of colourful soft corals, whip corals, sponges and gorgonians. Living on and adjacent to this wall is an impressive collection of fishes.

Schools of pelagic fish constantly patrol Perpendicular Wall. In the blue are always Rainbow Runners and a variety of batfish, trevally, barracuda, fusiliers and mackerel. Reef sharks regularly cruise the wall, but unfortunately most are shy of divers and keep their distance. This wall also attracts more impressive ocean wanderers, so keep an eye out for Whale Shark, Oceanic Manta Ray, Scalloped Hammerhead and even marlin.

On the wall itself is a wonderful assortment of fishes, including dense schools of Pyramid Butterflyfish and Black Triggerfish. Masses of basslets provide additional colour with several species seen here, including the very pretty Princess Basslet.

Princess Basslet (*Pseudanthias smithvanizi*).

Eibl's Angelfish (*Centropyge eibli*).

A wide variety of wrasses, goatfish, surgeonfish, scorpionfish, parrotfish, cardinalfish, squirrelfish, rockcods, blennies, hawkfish and damsels populate this wall. Sharp-eyed divers will spot Leaf Scorpionfish, Longnose Hawkfish and Bicolor Blenny.

A good number of endemic Cocos Pygmy Angelfish are seen on the wall, mostly in pairs darting in and out of holes. Divers are also likely to see Regal, Threespot and if you are lucky a small and rare Eibl's Angelfish. This cute little angelfish is only found in the Indian Ocean, and is known to crossbreed with the Pearlscale Angelfish to produce hybrids. And even stranger, this species also has a mimic, with juvenile Indian Ocean Mimic Surgeonfish copying its colour pattern. Why they do this is unknown, as most mimics copy poisonous fish to keep predators away.

Like other sites at Christmas Island, morays are a feature of this wall. Both

Whitemouth and Yellowmargin Morays pop up in unexpected places. However, the stars at this site are the Masked Morays. Not seen on the mainland, these eels are a little more aggressive than the average moray, lunging out at passing fish and divers. After watching this behaviour several times, I couldn't work out if these morays are cranky, curious or just a little short-sighted. Masked Morays are seen in large numbers on this wall, and generally in groups. If you find one, stop and look around it, as there are likely to be another six or more in the nearby holes.

Masked Moray (*Gymnothorax breedeni*).

99 THE RIP, COCOS (KEELING) ISLANDS

L ocated halfway between Western Australia and Sri Lanka are two remote coral atolls called the Cocos (Keeling) Islands. This external Australian territory is an island paradise that few people visit. Surrounded by blue water and extensive coral gardens these islands are a great place to fishwatch.

The southern atoll is where the airport and small towns are located, while the northern atoll is rarely visited. Only West and Home Islands are inhabited on the southern atoll – the other 25 islands are home to birds, lizards and crabs. There are dozens of great spots to scuba dive around the southern atoll, unfortunately when I visited the dive operation was out of action. However, I was still able to snorkel and fishwatch.

The first area I snorkelled was around Direction Island, exploring a shipwreck and a wonderful manta ray cleaning station. However, the fish life in The Rip was more impressive. Located at the southern end of Direction Island is a channel that is constantly flushed with water. You simply jump in and go for a fast-paced ride as the current pushes you into the lagoon.

Only 4m deep, the main channel has a pretty coral garden on the southern side and many ledges to explore. Swimming in the current are trevally, barracuda, parrotfish, drummers and Blacktip Reef Shark. Groups of Powderblue Tang also sweep through here. These lovely fish are only found in the Indian Ocean, but unfortunately not off Western Australia, so it is a real treat to see them. They grow to 23cm in length and often form into large schools, feeding on algae they pick off the coral and rocks. These tangs are a type of surgeonfish, and like other members of the family they have a sharp blade at the base of their tail for defence.

Many fish shelter under the ledges, including coral snappers, sweetlips,

Powderblue Tang (*Acanthurus leucosternon*).

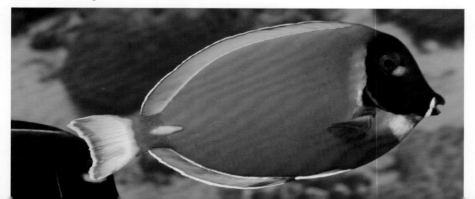

Birdwire Rockcod (*Epinephelus merra*).

squirrelfish and Whitetip Reef Shark. Moving to the coral gardens, where there is less current, you will see a wide variety of damsels, butterflyfish, wrasses, goatfish, surgeonfish, angelfish, coral snappers and pufferfish. Many Birdwire Rockcods rest between the corals. These small gropers have a pretty honeycomb pattern and grow to 35cm long. They are ambush predators, and sit casually on the bottom waiting for small crustaceans and fish to come within range to be grabbed.

The northern side of the channel is more barren, with only the occasional coral outcrop. However, you will need to snorkel over this zone to get back to Direction Island. Looks can be deceiving, as this area is home to gobies, damsels, surgeonfish, parrotfish, grubfish and many other species. This is a good spot to see a very attractive reef fish, the Lagoon Triggerfish. This widespread tropical species is nearly always seen in shallow lagoons, so mostly encountered by snorkellers. They live in holes in the bottom, which they retreat to when threatened, like when a snorkeller gets too close. They often go head-first into their home, which means they have to back out to exit, which is the best time to snap a photo. This species grows to 25cm in length, although juveniles, less than 5cm long, can also be seen in this area.

Lagoon Triggerfish (*Rhinecanthus aculeatus*).

The final fishwatching spot is also the shallowest site in this book, with the water around West Cay only 10cm to 2m deep, so a perfect spot for snorkelling. Located at the bottom end of West Island is a tiny palm-tree studded island called West Cay. The southern end of this cay has a shallow lagoon that is a haven for fishes.

To get to West Cay you need to first wade across a shallow channel, that often has a strong current between tides. Arriving on West Cay you will find a picturesque lagoon, bordered by a rocky ridge, that is sheltered from the current. This lagoon teems with schooling fish, including Blacktail Coral Snapper, Convict Surgeonfish, Yellowstripe Goatfish, Crocodile Longtom and Sea Mullet. The fish are often parted when a Bluefin Trevally or a Blacktip Reef Shark cruises through.

There are several ledges to investigate in this lagoon, where squirrelfish, soldierfish and cardinalfish hide. These ledges are also home to small groups of Lined Monocle Bream. Monocle breams are also called spinecheeks, as they have a spine below the eye. This is predominantly a tropical species, and often gets overlooked as it is not

Lined Monocle Bream (*Scolopsis lineata*).

Peppered Moray (*Gymnothorax pictus*).

as colourful as most reef fishes. Lined Monocle Bream grow to 25cm in length and feed on a range of small invertebrates.

Another fish found sheltering in these ledges is the Peppered Moray. This attractive eel is rarely seen by divers, as it generally lives on reef flats in water less than 1m deep. It grows to 1.2m long and likes to feed on crabs, even leaving the water to do so.

The main lagoon is a mix of coral, rubble and sand, and as such has a great variety of reef fishes. You will see an assortment of butterflyfish, wrasses, sandperch, triggerfish, gobies, blennies, damsels and pufferfish. There is even a small group of endemic Cocopeel Angelfish residing on one coral head.

I also spotted numerous juvenile fish sheltering in this lagoon, with a standout being several beautiful Indian Sailfin Tangs. This is another species only seen in the Indian Ocean, and not off mainland Australia. Adults grow to 40cm long, are seen in pairs and have a lovely striped and spotted pattern, while the juveniles have stripes and oversized fins, like they are going to grow into them. These fish feed on algae, plankton and even sea jellies.

You can easily spend several hours marvelling at all the wonderful reef fish in this lagoon. However, I would recommend you end your snorkel in the shallows on the far side of the island to see baby sharks. This spot seems to be a nursery area for juvenile Blacktip Reef Sharks – dozens of them. If you lie quietly on the bottom the little sharks, most are only 20cm to 30cm long, will slowly swim around you, getting closer and closer as they build up their confidence. It is an incredible experience and a wonderful way to end a fishwatching adventure.

Juvenile Indian Sailfin Tang (*Zebrasoma desjardinii*).

GLOSSARY

Barbel Fleshy tentacle extension near the mouth.

Benthic Bottom dwelling.

Bioluminescent Emission of light by living animals.

Bommie Short for bombora, being either a coral or rocky head or pinnacle.

Cephalopod Class of molluscs including the octopus, cuttlefish and squid.

Crustacean Hard-shelled animals such as crabs, shrimps and lobsters.

Diurnal Active by day.

Elasmobranch Class of fish, the sharks and rays.

Endemic Restricted to a certain area, state or country.

Hermaphrodite Animal having both female and male reproductive organs.

Invertebrate Animals that lack a backbone.

Mimicry The act of an animal copying the features or colours of another animal.

Molluscs Phylum of animals that typically have a foot and shell, like sea shells and snails.

Nocturnal Active by night.

Pelagic Inhabiting open water.

Plankton Small organisms, both plant and animal, that drift with ocean currents.

Syngnathidae Fish family containing seahorses, pipefish and seadragons.

Tunicate Marine invertebrate group including sea squirts and salps.

Zooplankton Small animal organisms that drift with ocean currents.

INDEX OF COMMON NAMES

INDEX OF SCIENTIFIC NAMES

First published in 2023 by Reed New Holland Publishers
Sydney

Level 1, 178 Fox Valley Road, Wahroonga, NSW 2076, Australia

newhollandpublishers.com

A record of this book is held at the National Library of Australia.

ISBN 978 1 92107 318 2

Managing Director: Fiona Schultz
Publisher and Project Editor: Simon Papps
Designer: Andrew Davies
Production Director: Arlene Gippert
Printed in China

10 9 8 7 6 5 4 3 2 1

Also available from Reed New Holland:

A Guide to Sea Fishes of Australia
Rudie H. Kuiter
ISBN 978 1 92554 680 4

Diving With Sharks
Nigel Marsh and Andy Murch
ISBN 978 1 92554 696 5

Green Guide: Sea Fishes of Australia
Nigel Marsh
ISBN 978 1 92554 638 5

Living Offshore Reefs of Australian Marine Parks
Graham Edgar, Rick Stuart-Smith and Antonia Cooper
ISBN 978 1 92554 686 6

*Muck Diving:
A diver's guide to the wonderful world of critters*
Nigel Marsh
ISBN 978 1 92151 781 5

*Tropical Marine Life of Australia:
Plants and Animals of the central Indo-Pacific*
Graham Edgar
ISBN 978 1 92151 758 7

*Tropical Marine Fishes of Australia:
A guide for waters from Rottnest Island to Lord Howe Island*
Rick Stuart-Smith, Graham Edgar, Andrew Green and Ian Shaw
ISBN 978 1 92151 761 7

Temperate Marine Life of Australia
Graham Edgar
ISBN 978 1 92151 717 4

*Underwater Australia:
The Best Dive Sites Down Under*
Nigel Marsh
ISBN 978 1 92151 792 1

*Wild Dives:
The most mind-blowing dives with marine animals from around the world*
Nick and Caroline Robertson-Brown
ISBN 978 1 92554 642 2

For details of hundreds of other Natural History titles see newhollandpublishers.com

Keep up with Reed New Holland and New Holland Publishers

 ReedNewHolland
 @NewHollandPublishers
and @ReedNewHolland